D1304084

THE GREAT CHICAGO MELTING POT COOKBOOK

Donated from the
Culinary Library of

Connie Ferrone

THE GREAT CHICAGO MELTING POT COOKBOOK

Agnes M. Feeney
and John L. Leckel

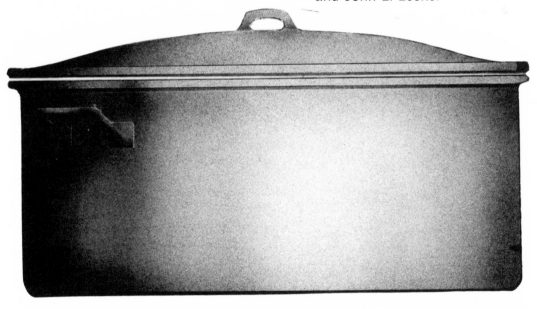

The Donning Company/Publishers
Virginia Beach/Norfolk

edcul
WISSER MEMORIAL LIBRARY

TX 725
.A1
9718
1980
c.1

Copyright © 1980 by Agnes M. Feeney and John L. Leckel

All rights reserved, including the right to reproduce this book in any form whatsoever without permission in writing from the publisher, except for brief passages in connection with a review. For information, write: The Donning Company/Publishers, 5041 Admiral Wright Road, Virginia Beach, Virginia 23462.

Printed in the United States of America

Table of Contents

List of Illustrations

Preface

The research undertaken in this work was both fascinating and rewarding because we searched out the heart of Chicago through its cuisines and cultures. We did not include all of the nationalities which make up this polyglot city, for there are literally hundreds of ethnic groups represented today. Each has its own uniqueness of character, culture and contribution to the Chicago style; we regret that neither time nor space allowed us to include all of them. We have attempted to focus on twenty nationalities or nationality groupings whose descendents now reside in Chicago and represent the major portion of its population.

The figures used in *The Great Chicago Melting Pot Cookbook* account for only foreign-born immigrants and first-generation Americans. Later generations which cling to the food heritages of their nationalities may still live in close proximity to each other and share similar cultural patterns, but are, for all practical purposes, considered to be Americans in census figures. Consequently, the actual number of people who identify with particular nationalities is far greater than the statistics imply.

The recipes used here reflect two significant features of the people from whom we received them. On the one hand, recipes were adapted to the availability of ingredients over the years, while on the other, the recent resurgence of interest in food heritage has occasioned adjustments in recipes to recapture their original character. Where possible we compared the recipes with their classical originals to determine how they had changed. What we discovered, in most cases, was that Melting Pot Cookery was just that, and, like *pizza,* was as American as apple pie. Goat and mutton appear nowhere on these pages; both have been displaced with lamb by the descendents of the immigrants. That spirit of change holds true for most of the ingredients. Where we had two or more recipes for the same dish, the variance between them often proved to be only in the method of preparation or in the amounts of seasoning—we found that the dish was essentially the same when completed, sometimes different from the classical version and sometimes not.

We have collected these recipes over a twenty-five year period. Some of them were given to us by people who have moved to other parts of the country, while others are reminders of those who are no longer with us. Many of the recipes have come to us from natives of the city who are alive and well and now living in Chicago or its environs. Where the recipe has not become our own through use, we have given the name of the generous individual who passed it along to us. To those whose names we have forgotten, we apologize.

We have made no attempt to explain basic cooking techniques and terminology. The user of this book who is not familiar with them should refer to any one of a number of basic cookbooks which detail and define techniques and terms.

We wish to thank Wynne Feeney, Joseph Feeney, and Dr. Clyde E. Robbins for their unstinting advice and encouragement, and Margaret Keefe and Mary Bridges of the Oak Park Library for their helpful searching and suggestions. The Indian Consulate, Yugoslavian Consulate, and British Consulate were extremely helpful in our search for festivals. To Judy Solomon, who typed and who often made order out of chaos, special thanks. For their help with recipes and ingredients we also wish to thank Reverend Ron Miyamura, Fred Bremer, Margaret Leckel, Alice O'Donnell, Fernando Capdevielle, Helen Below Capdevielle, Lockwood E. Wiley, Arlene Watson, Susan O'Connor, Martha Mack, John Vespo, Anthony Jandacek, Minton Ostertag, Corinne Leskovar, Rita Turner, Jasna Pavlouski, Kristina Allan, Rosemary Princ, T. M. Tali, Kenneth Brooks, Aldona Gallo, Louis Szathmary, Charles and Mary Marinko, Steven R. Zielinski, Father Alexander Cutler, Father Kollistus Langerholz, Dr. Grace Mabbu Parthasarathy, Kathy Kobus, and finally all those people who over the years gave us the recipes.

Introduction

Chicago is located on a stretch of land which was integral to the exploration of the western United States. By walking and floating only nine miles over the Chicago Portage, the late sixteenth and early seventeenth century explorers, fur trappers and missionaries could travel by water from the great waterways of the East to those of the Mississippi System. This strategic geographical location was elemental to Chicago's development.

The Chicago Portage was nearly forgotten for one hundred years until early in the nineteenth century, when a few trade centers were established at the newly built Fort Dearborn, and European settlers began to trickle in. With the establishment of Fort Dearborn, it seemed that the fledgling village at the river forks was well on its way. But the devastating destruction of the fort and many of its inhabitants in an Indian massacre turned the little outpost into a memory, and Chicago again became simply a place on the map in the midst of a woodland wilderness.

In the spirit that was to so characterize Chicago, a new fort was built within five years. With the construction of the new Fort Dearborn, many of the previous settlers whose lives had been spared returned. The regenerated little settlement soon began to draw immigrants from abroad and from other parts of the populated United States.

As Chicago moved into the third decade of the nineteenth century, its community grew, and the opening of the Erie Canal brought an even greater flood of immigrants to its lake shores. But the pattern that was so sharply drawn with its first great tragedy and subsequent recovery was to be repeated. The Indian's vengeance was visited again on the growing town, and the undrained swampy lands bred cholera epidemics. Each time disaster struck, the little village was staggered by the impact, but somehow managed to rise like the phoenix and rebuild, drawing more and more eager immigrants to it. Turning destruction into bigger and better reconstruction, and panic into economic boom, the insignificant village at the edge of Lake Michigan and between the forks of the Chicago River began to rival and outstrip many of the older and more established cities.

When Chicago became a city in 1837, a city census calculated the population at 4,710. Finally, the little Indian encampment with its inauspicious beginnings had launched its legend as a haven for new Americans who were frenetically trying to better their conditions and to make their fortunes in this new and unknown land.

And the world came to Chicago. As soon as the Illinois-Michigan Canal was constructed, Chicago became the hub of expansion: agricultural commodities passed through it on the way east, and people setting off to tame the wild country passed through it on the way west. Chicago was the door to the future and was wide open. In spite of depressions and panics, fires and famines, the city grew and expanded. "Urbs in Horto" became its motto, and the "I will" spirit its theme.

To this day, Andrew Greeley's observation, "You have to poke around the neighborhoods to know Chicago," is a fact. For in the neighborhoods are the people from all over the world who cling to the ethnic differences which give Chicago its flavor. The wealth of ethnic diversity has resulted in a city so rich in cuisines and combinations of cuisines that nowhere on the face of the earth can one travel where he may indulge in so incredible an array of gastronomic wonders in so small a geographical area.

THE GREAT CHICAGO MELTING POT COOKBOOK

The Black Americans

Chicago's first settler, Jean Baptiste Pointe du Sable, was a Black of Haitian and French Canadian parentage. The du Sable Trading Post was visited by many of the early French explorers who stopped at the Chicago Portage on their travels over the inland waterways of America.

There were sixty-five Black Americans living in Chicago in 1840, clustered around the south branch of the Chicago River. Early members of this community established several churches, the most remarkable of which was the Quinn Chapel, which served as a key station on the Underground Railroad and was founded in the mid-1840s. The first Black-owned business was a tailor shop located at the intersection of what is now Madison and Wells Streets. Its proprietor, John Jones, became an articulate leader of the Black community and one of its first members to be elected to public office. Other members of the community owned groceries, lumber stores, barbershops and a restaurant.

The first Black military unit in Illinois was organized in Chicago, and went on to fight in the Civil War with other Chicago-based ethnic units.

Although the numbers in the Black community grew steadily, the most significant increase in its population occurred during the World War I years. Chicago needed workers for the expanding rail and steel industries which were keeping pace with the city's growth and, like the early German and Irish immigrants to Chicago, Blacks were recruited from the states bordering Illinois by agents sent from the two giant industries. By 1920 the Black population numbered 109,500 and spread to the south and near west sides; *The Chicago Defender* was clearly on its way to becoming a nationally recognized Black newspaper and,

The House and Trading Post of Jean Baptiste Pointe du Sable which was located on the north bank of the Chicago River

most important, many of the sons and daughters of the Black community had entered business, education, medicine, law and politics.

In 1970, with a population of 1,100,000, the Black community outnumbered all of the foreign-born and first-generation ethnic groups combined. One of its greatest legacies, Jazz Chicago-style, is a bequest that is shared by Chicago with the world.

Black cuisine is a polyphony of "down-home" cooking. It is partly a peasant cuisine and partly a mélange of Southern aristocratic fare. Many of the techniques and ingredients have become commonplace in the repertoire of Chicago cooks of other ethnic backgrounds.

CORN BREAD

Yield: 6 to 8 servings

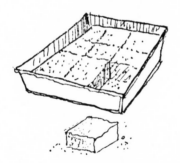

1 cup cornmeal
1 cup flour
1½ teaspoons baking powder
1 teaspoon salt
1 egg
3 tablespoons honey
1 cup milk, scant
¼ cup bacon drippings

Preheat oven to 425 degrees F.

Sift together the dry ingredients. Beat the egg until lemon-colored; beat in honey. Add milk to the egg, then mix with dry ingredients, adding the bacon drippings last. Beat until smooth. Bake in an 8-inch buttered or oiled pan for 25 minutes.

—Ann Eaton

WILTED LETTUCE

Yield: 4 servings

leaf lettuce, enough for 4 servings
4 scallions
8 strips bacon
¼ cup vinegar
¼ cup sugar
salt and pepper

Chop the lettuce coarsely and add the cut up scallions, place in serving dishes. Fry the bacon crisp and remove from skillet. Turn down heat to low, add the vinegar, sugar, salt and pepper and stir until sugar is dissolved. Pour over lettuce. Crumple two pieces of bacon over each serving.

TURNIP GREENS

Yield: 6 servings

4 bunches of turnip leaves and
   tender stems
1 clove garlic, minced
2 teaspoons sugar
pepper

¾ pound cut up salt pork or leftover smoked ham
salt, if needed
1 egg, hard-boiled

Wash and pick over greens, discarding tough stems. Chop greens and boil them in 2 quarts water with garlic, sugar, pepper and pork. When tender, drain and serve mounded on a platter, garnished with chopped hard-boiled egg.

—*Sammy Chester*

HOCKS AND BEANS

Yield: 4 servings

1 pound dried navy beans (red beans may be used)
4 quarts water
1 large onion, diced
1 large turnip, diced
1 large carrot, diced
1 bay leaf
4 smoked ham hocks or leftover baked ham and bones
salt and pepper

Wash beans and soak them for several hours. Drain, and bring them to a boil in 4 quarts of water. Add onion, turnip, carrot, bay leaf. After boiling for 40 minutes, add the hocks. Simmer for about 2½ hours or until thick and beans are soft, stirring occasionally. Add pepper; salt very lightly. Remove bay leaf before serving.

—Icie Babbs

FRIED CATFISH

Yield: 6 servings

2 eggs
¼ cup milk
6 8- to 10-inch catfish, prepared for cooking
¾ cup cornmeal
¾ cup flour
salt and pepper
vegetable oil for frying

Beat the eggs and the milk together. In separate bowl, combine the cornmeal and flour. Dip the catfish in the egg mixture, then in the cornmeal mixture. Place in a skillet with 1 inch of hot oil in it, and fry on each side until golden. Do not overfry, or fish will be dry.

In the 1850s, one of Chicago's most successful restaurants was Ambrose's and Jackson's. The two men had escaped slavery, could neither read nor write, but were superlative cooks.

MASHED SWEET POTATOES

Yield: 6 to 8 servings

6 sweet potatoes, cooked
3 eggs, beaten
1 teaspoon grated orange rind
1 teaspoon orange juice
⅓ cup brown sugar
¼ cup (½ stick) butter
½ cup milk
salt
1 teaspoon baking powder

Preheat oven to 350 degrees F.
Peel and mash the potatoes. Add all of the other ingredients and beat until fluffy. Place in buttered 2-quart casserole dish and bake for 35 minutes or until slightly browned.

CRAB CAKES

Yield: 8 servings

1 onion, grated
1 green pepper, finely diced
1 tablespoon butter
2 cups bread crumbs
1 egg

3 tablespoons cream
salt and pepper
1 pound cooked crab meat
oil or fat for deep frying

Sauté onion and green pepper in butter until soft. Place in large bowl with crumbs, egg, cream, salt and pepper and mix well. Add crab meat and form into cakes, adding more cream if necessary to bind. Fry in deep fat. Serve with tartar sauce.

"Bet your bottom dollar you'll lose your blues in Chicago"

OXTAILS

Yield: 4 servings

24 oxtail segments
½ cup flour
¼ cup (½ stick) butter, generous
½ cup carrots, finely diced
½ cup onions, finely diced
½ cup celery, finely diced

1 quart water, or enough to cover
4 medium tomatoes, peeled and chopped
½ teaspoon allspice
salt and pepper

Dredge the oxtail segments in flour and brown well in butter; remove from pan. Add the aromatics and saute until soft. Return the oxtails. Add water, tomatoes and spice. Simmer for 1½ to 2 hours until tender. Serve with rice.

PORK CHOPS IN WHITE GRAVY

Yield: 6 servings

½ cup flour
6 pork chops
1 egg, beaten

6 tablespoons bacon grease
1 pint cream
salt and pepper

Place half the flour in a shallow container. Dip the chops in flour, then in egg, and again in flour. Fry in bacon grease until done; remove to a warm platter. Make a roux with the remaining flour and the bacon grease in the pan, adding a little more grease if necessary. Add the cream, salt and pepper and stir until thickened, scraping the pan of bits of chops. Serve the gravy over the chops.

Grits and hominy, derived from corn, have been important to the diet of both Blacks and American Indians. Versatile, indeed, is the native grain which forms the basis for bread, candy, desserts and whiskey.

BLACK CHERRY UPSIDE-DOWN CAKE

Yield: 6 to 8 servings

¼ cup (½ stick) butter, unsalted
¾ cup brown sugar
36 black cherries, halved and pitted
1 cup twice sifted flour
2 teaspoons baking powder
dash of salt
2 eggs, separated
1 cup granulated sugar
6 tablespoons hot water
1 teaspoon vanilla

Preheat oven to 350 degrees F.

Melt butter in a 10- to 12-inch spider (cast-iron skillet). Add brown sugar and cook until sugar is dissolved and mixture is bubbly and slightly thickened. Take off the heat and place cherry pieces evenly throughout the mixture. In a large bowl, sift together dry ingredients. Beat egg yolks until thick and add to dry ingredients. Beat in granulated sugar, hot water and vanilla. Beat egg whites stiff and fold in; pour over butter mixture in spider. Bake for 40 minutes or until toothpick inserted in cake comes out clean. Remove from oven and let cool ten minutes. Place cake plate over spider and, using both hands, invert cake onto plate; gently remove spider.

The Bud Billikan Parade is the third largest parade in the United States. There are 160 floats and 125,000 participants. The first parade was held in 1924 in Washington Park to honor newsboys who distributed *The Chicago Defender*. The parade is named after a fictitious newsboy whose likeness is portrayed in a gigantic balloon replica which leads the festivities. The purpose of this spectacular affair is to raise money and collect food for the poor.

The Chinese

Early Chinese immigrants came to Chicago by way of California after having worked on the railroad systems in the far West. In 1890, a small community of these newcomers settled near Van Buren and Clark Streets. At the turn of the century the little community became crowded with new arrivals because of the persistent expansion of businesses in the central city area. Most of these Chinese-Chicagoans moved to the area that is now known as Chinatown, and by 1920 there were almost 2,000 inhabitants in this area.

Chinatown, which is located at 22nd Street and Wentworth Avenue, is dominated by the Chinese City Hall, a three-story building charmingly decorated with oriental motifs. Although several religious centers and St. Theresa's Mission are close by, it is the Chinese City Hall which serves as the center for social and civic affairs in Chinatown.

Shops with exotic and wonderfully mysterious foodstuffs line the streets. Merchants sell their wares of clothing made of luxurious fabrics executed in meticulous oriental fashion; others display art objects, delicate dishes and cooking utensils. Restaurants of fine quality abound, and most Chicagoans are not strangers to them.

By 1975, 8,000 Chinese-Americans had settled in Chicago. Many have remained in the old area of Chinatown, but a great number of sons and daughters, grandsons and granddaughters of those first immigrants have scattered throughout the city adding their talents to the artistic, educational and professional development of the city's culture.

The Chinese indeed have contributed to the grand array of food heritages which make up the city. Most European-Americans are familiar with Chinese food through restaurant and "take-home" establishments. But wok-stir-fry cookery has become so popular that many occidental Chicago cooks have become adept at preparing this simple but exquisite cuisine from the East.

Gate at entrance to Chinatown at 22nd and Wentworth

BARBECUED SPARERIBS

Yield: 10 to 12 servings

2½ pounds spareribs, cut in 3-inch
   pieces and boiled for 1 hour in
   salted water
1½ cups soy sauce
3 tablespoons sherry

3 tablespoons brown sugar
1 onion, diced
3 cloves garlic, crushed
5 tablespoons honey
2½ tablespoons soy sauce

Marinate ribs in a mixture of the next 5 ingredients for 8 hours. Bake for 30 minutes in oven that has been preheated to 400 degrees F. Paint ribs with a mixture of honey and remaining soy sauce and bake for 8 minutes longer. Serve hot as hors d'oeuvres.

SPRING ROLLS

Yield: 12 rolls

cold water (keep cold by adding ice
   cubes)
6 cups flour
4 tablespooons peanut oil
2 scallions, white and green parts,
   cut in strips
½ pound chicken, uncooked, cut in
   strips
3 cups bean sprouts
3 cups bok choy, chopped
¾ cup dried mushrooms, plumped
   in water and squeezed, cut in
   strips
1 cup shrimp, chopped
3½ tablespoons soy sauce
2½ tablespoons sherry
salt and pepper
MSG, pinch
fat or oil for deep frying

Mix icy cold water with flour until a soft dough is formed. Roll out very thin and cut in 5-inch rectangles. Heat the oil in a skillet. Fry scallions until soft; add the chicken and fry until white. Pour boiling water over the bean sprouts; drain, then add to skillet. Add the bok choy and mushrooms; stir for 4 minutes. Add the shrimp and stir for 3 minutes. Stir in sauce made of the rest of ingredients and stir for 2 minutes. Fill each dough rectangle with 2½ tablespoons of mixture. Roll up and tuck in ends, sealing with a mixture of flour and water. Fry in 3 inches of deep fat until golden, drain on paper towels.

HOT AND SOUR SOUP

Yield: 6 servings

4½ cups canned chicken broth
½ cup pork, cut in strips
½ cup chicken breast, cut in strips
6 dried black mushrooms, plumped in water and squeezed, cut in strips
1 tablespoon salt
½ cup lemon juice

2 teaspoons pepper
2 slices ginger, diced
2 scallion whites (save green tops for garnish)
1½ tablespoons soy sauce
3 tablespoons cornstarch
4 tablespoons broth

Bring broth to the boil; add pork, chicken, mushrooms and simmer 8 minutes. Add salt, juice, pepper, ginger, scallions, and soy sauce and simmer 8 minutes more. Mix cornstarch and broth and thicken soup with it. Serve with green scallion garnish.

ORIENTAL SALAD

Yield: 4 servings

1 cup chicken, cooked and cut in strips
2 cups bean sprouts
2 scallion whites, cut in strips

1 tablespoon soy sauce
1 tablespoon sherry
salt and pepper
1 tablespoon peanut oil

Mix chicken and vegetables. Make a sauce of the other ingredients and pour over chicken and vegetables. Serve very cold garnished with shredded scallion tops.

Stir Fry

When stir frying, Chinese equipment is fun but not necessary. You may use a wok, an electric fry pan, or a flat bottomed skillet; a wooden spoon or spatula will be as effective for stirring as anything else. Four tablespoons of peanut oil is the cooking medium. The basic rule is to fry the spices and flavoring in the oil, then the other ingredients, starting with the meat and ending with the more delicate vegetables. The final saucing is usually four tablespoons of soy sauce to one teaspoon of cornstarch. A tablespoon of sherry may be used in place of one of soy sauce. A teaspoon of bead molasses or sugar may be added without changing the amount of liquid in proportion to cornstarch. A pinch of monosodium glutamate (MSG) is usually added also. Have all ingredients prepared for frying, the sauce mixed, and the heat high. Stir constantly.

CHICKEN WITH PEA POD
AND BLACK MUSHROOM

Yield: 4 servings

peanut oil
2 scallions or one small onion
1 piece ginger, diced
1 clove garlic, crushed
1 chicken breast, boned
½ cup dried black mushrooms, plumped in water and squeezed
1½ cups pea pods, stemmed and washed
sauce (see **Stir Fry**)

Cut everything in strips, except the pea pods. In peanut oil, fry white part of scallions, ginger and garlic. Add chicken and fry about 6 minutes until cooked through, but not too browned. Add mushrooms and fry until hot; add pea pods and fry until hot. Add sauce, stirring until thick. Garnish with green scallion tops. Serve. Cooking time is about 12 minutes.

PORK WITH BEAN SPROUT

Yield: 4 servings

¾ pound bean sprouts
¾ pound pork, cut into strips
Bead molasses or ½ teaspoon sugar

Place sprouts in colander and pour boiling water over them. Dry them on toweling. Follow recipe for **Chicken with Pea Pod and Black Mushroom,** except fry pork strips 10 minutes or until no longer pink. Use bead molasses or sugar in sauce.

BEEF WITH BOK CHOY

Yield: 4 servings

¾ pound beef, cut in strips
4½ cups bok choy, cut on the
   diagonal

Follow directions for **Chicken with Pea Pod and Black Mushroom,** except cook beef just until brown and bok choy for 3 to 4 minutes.

Late in the nineteenth century, hunters sold their wares to meat commission houses on South Water Street. Quail, prairie chicken, partridge, teal, jacksnipe and grouse went for two dollars a dozen.

Remembered food: Sunday meals at Grandma's, and Mother's special dishes; food that reminds us of another place, some other time. That's what these delightful recipes are. They are not anyone's everyday fare. Everyday food is meat, potatoes and vegetables. These dishes are like a spool of culinary memories that bring back good times and family conviviality. They palpably link us to our past.

STEWED DUCK

Yield: 4 servings

3 tablespoons peanut oil
1 large duck, cut into serving pieces
3 scallions, cut in strips
1 clove garlic, mashed
1 slice ginger, diced
¾ cup soy sauce

2½ tablespoons sherry
2 tablespoons brown sugar
½ teaspoon salt
2½ cups water
2 tablespoons cornstarch
4 tablespoons water

In a Dutch oven, heat the oil and brown duck pieces; pour off all fat. Add scallions, garlic and ginger, stir for 3 minutes. Add mixture of soy sauce, sherry, sugar and salt and stir 1 minute. Add water and simmer with lid for 2 hours. Thicken with paste made of cornstarch and water. Serve with scallion tops as garnish.

SHRIMP EGG FOO YUNG

Yield: 4 to 6 servings

6 eggs
3 tablespoons cornstarch
2 cups boiling water
½ cup bean sprouts
6 shrimp, cleaned and cut in strips
¼ cup dried mushrooms, plumped
    and squeezed, cut in strips
2 scallions
MSG, pinch
salt
8 tablespoons peanut oil

Beat eggs with cornstarch. Pour boiling water over bean sprouts in a colander and drain well; add to eggs. Add all other ingredients except oil and stir. Heat the oil in a skillet. Spoon mixture into skillet in pancake shapes; fry until set, then turn and fry other side. Serve. Using similar proportions and preparation, any combination may be added to the eggs: crab and bamboo shoots, chicken and ham, or pork.

FRIED RICE

Yield: 6 servings

3 cups rice
6 cups water
4 tablespoons peanut oil
1 cup pork, cut in matchstick strips
3 scallion whites, chopped
3 eggs, beaten
3 tablespoons soy sauce
1 tablespoon sherry
salt and pepper
MSG, pinch
1 tablespoon cornstarch

Wash the rice until the water runs clear. If rice is not washed thoroughly, it will be sticky when cooked. Add the rice and 6 cups water to large pot and simmer with lid on for 20 minutes. *Do not* lift the lid. When rice is cooked, cool to room temperature. Heat the oil in a large skillet. Add the pork and onions and stir until pork is done and onions soft. Add the eggs and rice and stir; cook for 4 minutes. Mix the soy sauce, sherry, salt, pepper, MSG and cornstarch, and add to the rice mixture; stir until blended. Garnish with scallion tops and serve. Keeping the same proportions, shrimp, peas, ham, beef or mushrooms may be added to the rice.

FRIED SHRIMP

Yield: 6 servings

2 tablespoons soy sauce
2 tablespoons sherry
salt and pepper
MSG, pinch
1 clove garlic, mashed

36 large shrimp, cleaned
3 eggs
2½ tablespoons cornstarch
2½ tablespoons flour
peanut oil for frying

Mix soy sauce, sherry, salt, pepper, MSG and garlic. Add the shrimp and marinate for 1 hour at room temperature. Mix the eggs, cornstarch and flour. Dip the shrimp into the batter and fry in 3 inches of peanut oil until golden. Drain on paper towels.

ALMOND COOKIES

Yield: 4 to 5 dozen

1 cup butter
2¼ cups flour
1¼ cups sugar
⅔ teaspoon baking soda

pinch of salt
2 eggs, beaten well
1½ tablespoons almond extract
¼ pound sliced almonds

Preheat oven to 325 degrees F.

Cut butter into dry ingredients and stir in the eggs and extract. Mix to a dough consistency. Roll out to ¼-inch thickness and cut with a 2-inch glass or cookie cutter. Place on a greased baking sheet and press 3 slices of almonds in a petal shape on each. Bake for 25 to 30 minutes.

Chinese New Year is celebrated in February in Chinatown at 22nd and Wentworth. A giant, people-filled dragon caroms through the streets greeting revellers as firecrackers explode to welcome in the new year. Chinese restaurants lining Wentworth Avenue have special dishes prepared to entice the hungry in to try their special celebratory delights. This festive occasion attracts Chicagoans in large numbers because of the joy of the observance and the wonderful foods which abound.

The city with the open arms

Museum of Science and Industry, 57th Street and South Lake Shore Drive

The Croatians, Serbians and Slovenians

Shifts in political ideologies and boundary changes of the countries of eastern Europe and the Balkan States caused waves of migration in the latter part of the nineteenth century. The immigrants who came from the Balkan States of the Austro-Hungarian Empire had emerged from agronomic backgrounds, but contributed their vigor and vitality to the complex industries and available employment in the teeming city. Although these groups of nationalities came from geographic origins which are similar, political differences kept them as distinct units.

By 1920, the composite population of these groups of foreign-born and first-generation Americans had reached almost one thousand.

The Croatians, who were mainly Roman Catholic, soon established population centers on the near and far south sides of Chicago. As with many other ethnic groups, the establishment of nationalistic churches was of primary concern to them. By 1920, two Croatian churches had been built in each of the two existing ethnic communities.

The Serbians, who were Orthodox Christians, began organizing small communities in Chicago in the latter part of the nineteenth century. Like those of the Croatians, these centers were near the places of employment of the community members. One settlement grew up on the near south side in the vicinity of the stock yards, while another developed on the far south side close to the steel mills.

The Slovenians first settled near Cermak Road and Wolcott Streets at the turn of the century. In 1904 they built St. Stephen's Roman Catholic Church and established the KSKJ, a Slovenian benefit association.

By 1970, the number of foreign-born and first generation Americans from these ethnic groups numbered almost 28,800. Although many are scattered over the entire city, the original ethnic population centers still bring early residents back to share their sense of nationalistic pride.

The cuisines of these nationalities are basically peasant in ingredients and preparation, yet a sophistication is lent to many of the dishes by the subtle influence of the eastern European and Slavic touches found in some of the recipes.

West side of St. Stephen's Church at 1852 W. 22nd Place

KOČAN LEB
(Corn Bread)

Yield: 6 servings

2½ cups cornmeal
½ teaspoon salt
3 eggs
½ cup melted butter
1 cup milk

Preheat oven to 350 degrees F.

Mix cornmeal and salt. Add eggs, butter and half the milk, beat and let rest for ten minutes. Add rest of milk and beat again. Butter an 8-by-8-inch baking dish and place batter in it. Bake for about 60 minutes until golden.

LAORAF LISTE
(Cauliflower Soup)

Yield: 6 servings

1 large cauliflower
1½ tablespoons butter
1½ tablespoons flour
2 quarts hot milk
salt and white pepper
6 tablespoons sour cream
1 lemon rind, grated

Cook the cauliflower until tender in salted water. Drain and break it in small pieces. Make a roux of the butter and flour in a large pot. Add the milk, salt and pepper, and bring to a simmer; add the cauliflower. When hot, ladle into serving bowls. Place a dollop of sour cream on each and sprinkle on the lemon rind.

PEČENI CELER
(Braised Celery)

Yield: 4 servings

1 large bunch celery
3 tablespoons butter
3 cups chicken stock, enough to
   cover celery
salt and pepper

Preheat oven to 375 degrees F.

Clean the celery and cut into 1-inch pieces. Melt the butter in a casserole dish and swirl the celery in. Add chicken stock, salt and pepper. Heat on top of stove until bubbly. Cover and bake in oven for 40 minutes until tender. Serve.

GLIVE SA JAJIMA I PAVLAKOM
(Cream, Mushrooms and Eggs)

Yield: 4 servings

1 onion, chopped
3 tablespoons butter
1½ pounds mushrooms, cleaned
   and sliced
5 eggs

1½ teaspoons flour
salt and pepper
¾ cup heavy cream
parsley, for garnish

Sauté the onion in the butter until soft. Add the mushrooms; sauté until golden. Beat eggs, flour and seasonings until frothy; add to mushrooms. Cover and cook until curdling, about 8 to 10 minutes. Stir and add cream. Simmer for 5 to 8 minutes, stirring once or twice. Serve with parsley garnish.

In response to a request from Chicago for a ten thousand dollar loan, Shawneetown, Illinois (today's population five hundred), wrote: "Chicago is too far from Shawneetown ever to amount to much."

DJUVEČE
(Lamb Chop Casserole)

Yield: 4 servings

4 onions, sliced
2½ tablespoons butter
4 lamb chops (pork chops may be used)
4 potatoes, sliced

4 tomatoes, sliced
2 green peppers, seeded and sliced
salt and pepper
2 cups tomato juice

Preheat oven to 350 degrees F.

Brown the onions in the butter. Sauté the chops in the same pan. Layer the potatoes, tomatoes and peppers in a buttered casserole dish; salt and pepper each layer, place the chops on the top, and pour the tomato juice over all. Bake for 45 minutes covered, and uncovered for 10 minutes.

JAGNEŠKO MESO SO KISELO MLEKO
(Veal in Sour Cream)

Yield: 4 servings

1 lemon
1 pound veal, cubed
1 yellow onion, chopped
1½ tablespoons butter
3 tablespoons flour
salt and white pepper
¾ cup beef broth
¼ cup sour cream

Squeeze the lemon over the veal and let stand 15 minutes. Sauté the onion in the butter until soft; add veal and brown. Sprinkle with the flour, salt and pepper; stir. Add broth and simmer for about 1 hour until tender. Swirl in sour cream and serve.

POLNATA KROMIT
(Filled Onions)

Yield: 6 servings

6 large onions	1 tablespoon flour
¾ pound ground lamb	1 tablespoon tomato paste
¼ cup cooked rice	⅔ cup sour cream
salt and pepper	hot water
6 tablespoons butter	vinegar

Preheat oven to 350 degrees F.

Parboil the onions. Remove a slice from the top of each and scoop out center. Mix the meat, rice, salt and pepper, and stuff the onions. Make a roux with the butter and flour, add the tomato paste, and stir. Add the sour cream and turn heat low. Add enough water to make a heavy sauce. Arrange the onions in a casserole dish and pour the sour cream gravy over them. Pour 1 inch of water into a pan larger than the casserole. Place the casserole dish in the pan of water, and bake for about 40 minutes. Sprinkle with vinegar and serve.

KOKOČKA GIGER SO KROMIT I PIPER
(Chicken Liver with Onions and Pepper)

Yield: 6 servings

1 large onion, diced	3 green peppers, seeded and diced
4 tablespoons chicken fat, divided	3 tomatoes, peeled and diced
1 pound chicken livers	salt and pepper
1½ tablespoons flour	

Sauté onion in 2 tablespoons of fat. Add livers and stir gently for 8 minutes. Spread flour over livers evenly and fry until well browned. In another pan, sauté peppers in 2 tablespoons of fat until soft; add tomatoes and salt and pepper. Add liver mixture and cook over low heat for 10 minutes longer, stirring occasionally. Serve.

"My kind of town: Chicago is!"

KOKOČKA SO KISELO MLEKO
(Chicken in Sour Cream)

Yield: 4 servings

1 frying chicken, cut up
3 cups sour cream
3 cloves garlic, mashed
salt and pepper

Boil the chicken in 3 quarts water for 30 minutes; drain. Place chicken in large skillet and cover with the sour cream. Add the garlic and salt and pepper, and simmer gently for 10 minutes.

ČEVAPČIČI
(Meat Rolls)

Yield: 4 servings

1½ pounds mixture of ground lamb
   and veal
1 large onion, chopped fine

½ teaspoon cumin
salt and pepper
4 tablespoons water

Mix all ingredients together and knead until paste-like. Roll into 2½-inch torpedo shapes. Thread onto skewers. Broil 10 to 12 minutes or until done.

Food is the great leveler. As one begins to appreciate a people's cuisine, he begins to understand the people: they become less mysterious, less different. One of the many reasons that "the city that works" works, is its broad appreciation and understanding of diverse food choices.

LEB SO SEJKER
(Sweet Loaves)

Yield: 18 loaves

3 eggs
1 cup sugar, generous
⅔ cup almonds, blanched and
   ground
¼ teaspoon cinnamon
¼ teaspoon allspice
2 tablespoons candied fruit,
   chopped fine
2 cups flour, depending on egg size

Preheat oven to 375 degrees F.

Beat the eggs and sugar together until sugar is completely absorbed into eggs and the mixture is pale yellow, about 12 minutes. Add all other ingredients but flour and mix. Add flour and knead dough in bowl until smooth. Shape into 18 loaves, 2-by-2-inches, and bake on a buttered cookie sheet for about 30 minutes until golden. Cool on sheets.

BLAGI JABOLKA
(Syrup Apples)

Yield: 6 servings

6 apples
5 cups water
1 cup sugar
1 lemon, juiced

6 tablespoons pear liqueur
12 tablespoons whipped cream
cinnamon

Peel and core the apples, leaving the stem end closed. Boil them gently in a mixture of water, sugar and lemon juice until tender, about 25 minutes. Drain and place in refrigerator until cold. When ready to serve, place on dessert plates, fill centers with pear liqueur, top with whipped cream, and sprinkle with cinnamon.

The Czechs

In the 1850s, Czech immigrants began to reach Chicago. Their numbers were estimated at five hundred when they took up temporary quarters in the vacant area just south of Lincoln Park, before being evicted by the owners of that property bordering the lake. They then settled in an area which is still known as "Praha," located between 12th, Harrison, Canal and Halsted Streets.

Like other immigrants from Europe, one of their initial goals was the establishment of a church where they might worship in their own language. The first Catholic Bohemian church, St. Wenceslaus, was built in 1866 at DeKoven and DesPlaines Streets. (Mrs. O'Leary and her cow lived on DeKoven Street, also.)

The Czech community demonstrated a tradition of nationalistic unity, although its members represented a wide range of political and religious ideologies. It is no wonder that by the turn of the century many members of this group were active and successful as members of government at the local, state and national levels.

As Chicago grew, so did the Czech population. The "Praha" area remained the center for Czech culture, but eventually communities were set up in Pilsen and in South Chicago near the steel mills. By 1870, there were more than 6,000 foreign-born Czechs in Chicago, and in 1930, 161,000 foreign-born and their children were living in the area.

Czech food, like Irish food, is a peasant cuisine. Goose and pork are the mainstays of the meat diet, and both were plentiful in the rapidly developing city on the lake. Sausage is the most popular of all Czech food, and its making has been referred to as an art. Many of the yeast breads and desserts brought by this hardy band of immigrants can be found in bakeries throughout the Chicago area.

Mother and daughter in traditional dress

SULC
(Pork in Aspic)

Yield: 8 servings

6 pork hocks, large size
4 pigs feet, large size
small clove of garlic

2 tablespoons pickling spices in
  cheese cloth bag
2 bay leaves

Place all ingredients in Dutch oven and add enough water to cover. Cook until meat falls from the bones. Strain the broth, and using just enough to cover, pour over the meat that has been cleaned from the bones and cut into pieces. Pour into a greased loaf pan and chill.

POLÉVKA S JÁTRA KNEDLÍĆKY
(Liver Dumpling Soup)

Yield: 6 servings

½ pound liver, ground
1 teaspoon softened butter
1 clove garlic, mashed
½ teaspoon crushed sage or
  marjoram
1 lemon rind, washed and grated
salt and pepper
1 egg
bread crumbs to make soft dough
1½ quarts chicken or beef broth
1 tablespoon chopped fresh
  parsley

Mix all ingredients well and form into walnut-size dumplings. Drop into 1½ quarts of simmering chicken or beef broth to which a tablespoon of chopped fresh parsley has been added; boil about 10 minutes.

HOUSKA
(Fruit Bread)

Yield: 6 to 8 servings

1 package dry yeast
1 tablespoon sugar
¼ cup warm water

Dissolve yeast and sugar in
warm water, in bowl.

⅓ cup milk, scalded
¼ cup sugar
¼ cup (½ stick) butter
1 teaspoon salt

Combine in large bowl; cool.
Add yeast mixture. Then add

2 eggs, beaten
½ teaspoon vanilla
½ teaspoon nutmeg
About 2½ cups sifted all-purpose
    flour to make stiff dough.

Turn out on floured board and knead with

1 cup diced candied fruit

until smooth and elastic. Place dough in a buttered bowl, cover and let
rise until doubled, about 1 hour. Knead dough for 30 seconds and let
rise again until doubled. Cut dough into three equal pieces. Roll each
piece with hands into a long strand about 18 inches long. Braid the
strands, and place braid in a large greased loaf pan or shallow 12-by-7-
by-2-inch baking dish. Sprinkle with almonds. Cover and let rise for 30
minutes.

    Bake for 40 minutes in oven that has been preheated to 350
degrees F. At the last 10 minutes of baking, brush braid with beaten
egg to which 1 teaspoon water has been added. Bake to golden brown.
Cool in pan 10 minutes; then turn Houska out onto a rack to cool—at
least 10 minutes—before slicing.

FAZOLE V KOPROVA OMACKA
(Green Beans with Dill Gravy)

Yield: 4 servings

2 tablespoons minced onion
2 tablespoons butter
2 tablespoons flour
2 cups milk
½ cup sour cream

¼ to ⅓ cup chopped fresh dill leaves
¼ teaspoon salt
dash of pepper
1 pound green beans cooked

Sauté onions in butter until golden brown. Add flour and mix together well. Add 2 cups milk, stirring constantly. Cook until mixture thickens to a white sauce. Add chopped dill, sour cream, and salt and pepper; mix well, slowly. Heat through, but *do not boil.* Add green beans to sauce and keep warm until ready to serve.

—Dolores Bliss

ZELÍ
(Sweet Sour Cabbage)

Yield: 4 to 6 servings

1 large size onion
1 tablespoon butter
1 head cabbage
1 cup water

1 tablespoon salt
1 teaspoon caraway seed
1½ tablespoons vinegar
1½ tablespoons sugar

Slice onion and sauté in butter until golden. Chop cabbage coarsely and place in 2-quart pot. Add sautéed onion, water, salt and caraway seed, cover and cook over low heat for about a half hour. When cabbage is tender, turn off heat, add sugar and stir until dissolved; add vinegar and stir thoroughly. Serve immediately.

NEW YORK INSTITUTE
OF TECHNOLOGY

DRUCH KVETAKU MICHANINA
(Broccoli Casserole)

Yield: 10 servings

6 eggs
2 pounds creamed cottage cheese
   (small curd)
6 tablespoons flour
½ pound diced processed cheese
1 10-ounce package frozen

chopped broccoli or ¾ pound
   fresh broccoli, chopped
¼ pound (1 stick) butter
2 chopped green onions, tops and
   all
1 tablespoon caraway seeds

Preheat oven to 350 degrees F.

Bring all ingredients to room temperature, then buzz in a blender until smooth. Pour into greased 9-by-12-inch baking dish, and bake for 1 hour, or until a knife comes out almost clean. Let rest at room temperature for 10 minutes before serving.

PLACKI
(Potato-Kraut Cakes)

Yield: 6 servings

4 large cooked potatoes
4 tablespoons (½ stick) butter
½ cup cream

1 cup canned sauerkraut which has
   been washed and drained
salt and pepper to taste
enough flour to bind ingredients

Mash potatoes with butter and cream. Add other ingredients, mix and form into pancakes. Fry in butter until golden brown, turn and fry other side. Drain on paper towels.

Jane Addams' Hull House was a center for newly arrived immigrants who received help until they became established in the community. Hull House has since become a shrine to many Chicago residents whose families received its aid.

KUBA
(Baked Barley Grits)

Yield: 4 to 6 servings

¾ cup finely chopped onion
¼ cup (½ stick) butter
1½ cups barley grits
1½ cups dried mushrooms
7 cups cold water

2 teaspoons salt
¼ teaspoon pepper
2 medium or 1 large clove garlic,
    pressed

Preheat oven to 350 degrees F.

Sauté the onion in the butter until transparent. Place grits, mushrooms, and salt in water and cook until water has evaporated, stirring frequently—the mixture will be very thick. Add remaining ingredients; place in a greased 2-quart baking dish and bake in oven about 30 to 35 minutes.

—Dorothy Svoboda

SALAT
(Meat Salad)

Yield: 4 servings

2 cups pork, roasted
1½ cups dill pickles
1 cup onion
1 cup sour apples
1 tablespoon lemon juice

1 teaspoon dill weed, chopped
salt and pepper
6 tablespoons mayonnaise, freshly
    made

Cut pork, pickles, onion and apples into 2-inch strips. Sprinkle with lemon juice, dill weed, salt and pepper and toss with mayonnaise. Serve chilled.

"Hog butcher of the world"

SVÍČKOVÁ
(Beef in Sour Cream Gravy)

Yield: 8 servings

3 pounds beef tenderloin
3 cups water
2½ cups wine vinegar
1 onion, sliced
2 bay leaves
12 whole cloves
½ teaspoon allspice
2 or 3 strips bacon
2 tablespoons flour
1 pint sour cream
salt

Place tenderloin in large bowl. Blend water, vinegar, onion, bay leaves, cloves and allspice; pour over beef. Let marinate for 2 days in refrigerator; turn meat occasionally. Drain marinade, strain and reserve. Preheat oven to 325 degrees F. Place meat in shallow pan (9-by-13-inch). Cover meat with strips of bacon; bake for 2 hours, basting occasionally with reserved liquid. Remove meat from pan and discard bacon. Slice meat into ½ inch slices; keep warm in a deep serving dish as you prepare gravy. Blend 2 tablespoons flour into sour cream with a whisk. If sour cream is thick, add a little water to make it the consistency of whipped cream. Strain marinade into roasting pan; heat to simmering, scraping pan. Gradually stir in sour cream mixture, blending well to make smooth gravy. Season to taste with salt. Pour over meat slices and serve.

Chicago is laid out in a grid pattern; however, some streets run counter to it. These were old Indian trails which the receding glacier of long before had left as smooth pathways: North Clark Street, Ridge and Vincennes Avenues, and most other diagonal streets.

VEPŘOVÍ A KNEDLÍKY
(Pork, Dumplings and Gravy)

Yield: 10 servings

6 pounds loin roast of pork
salt and pepper

1 teaspoon caraway seeds
2 onions, sliced in rings

Preheat oven to 325 degrees F.

Wipe roast with cloth. Sprinkle with salt, pepper and caraway seeds. Place, fat side up, on rack in open roasting pan. Roast in oven 35 minutes per pound, or until meat thermometer reads 185 degrees. Add onion one half hour before meat is done. Make gravy from juices in roasting pan, 6 tablespoons pork fat (drained from pan), 6 tablespoons flour, 1 teaspoon salt and 3 cups cold water.

Dumplings

1 cup sifted all-purpose flour
1 teaspoon salt
1½ teaspoons baking powder
1 egg

¼ cup milk
1 slice buttered toast, diced
1 teaspoon salt
3 quarts boiling water

Sift together dry ingredients. Break egg into milk, beat with fork to blend, and add to dry ingredients. Mix until well moistened. Add toast and mix. Shape into long roll, 3 inches in diameter. Add salt and dumpling to boiling water. Roll several times with fork to prevent sticking. Cover, and simmer 15 minutes, then simmer, uncovered, another 5 minutes. Remove with slotted spoon. Cut immediately into slices; serve.

A major Czech festival is held annually in the Cicero-Berwyn suburbs. Called Houby (Mushroom) Day, it occurs in the fall before the first frost, and consists of a parade, the crowning of a Houby Queen, sidewalk merchants, and a football game known as the Houby Bowl. The Czechs are gatherers of wild mushrooms. Most popular locally are Kotrc, a giant cauliflowerlike fungus, and Vaclavky, a bunched growth of fungi.

KINUTÝ ŠVESKOVÉ KNEDLÍČKY
(Raised Plum Dumplings)

Yield: 2 dozen dumplings

1 tablespoon sugar
1 package (¼ ounce) dry yeast
1 cup lukewarm milk
3 cups flour

3 eggs, beaten
1 teaspoon salt
24 canned plums

Add sugar and yeast to milk and stir. In a separate bowl, combine flour, eggs and salt. After yeast has risen, combine both mixtures and beat. Work well into a smooth dough. Place on a floured board and knead until thick. Put the dough back into the bowl and let rise until doubled, about 1 hour. Take dough from bowl and form into rolls about 2 inches in diameter. Cut into ½-inch pieces and flatten each piece of dough. Dip each plum into flour, place one on each piece of flattened dough, and press edges of dough firmly around plum. Allow the plum dumplings to rise. Place dumplings in boiling water for 10 minutes. Lift out with slotted spoon and immediately poke once with a fork. They may be sprinkled with butter, cottage cheese, and/or sugar. Instead of plums, peaches or apricots may be used.

—Agnes Kyndl

The East Indians

In 1870, the East Indian population of Chicago was registered at a scant eight individuals. Even by the turn of the century the members of this ethnic group barely numbered one hundred, and it was not until the mid-1960s that they began to arrive in the area in significant numbers. Population quota laws with political origins had prevented East Indians from settling in the United States and gaining citizenship, but with the relaxation of the laws under Presidents Kennedy and Johnson, the people from Southern Asia were encouraged to claim their portion of the American Dream.

By 1970, approximately three thousand East Indians and Pakistani and their children made up a segment of the Chicago population. Today many of them worship in churches whose missionaries had established Christian communities in their native land. Although the group is scattered throughout the Chicago area, there are clusters of East Indians and Pakistanis near the major hospital and university centers, for many of these individuals were brought to Chicago because of their outstanding abilities in these two professional areas. Indeed, unlike their immigrant predecessors a century before, most of these new Chicagoans have come from upper middle class professional families.

This group, too, clings to its national heritage, as evidenced in the establishment of mutual benefit associations such as The India League of America and the Pakistani American Association. And Chicago has benefited by the cultural additive provided by them. In addition to their more sober contributions to the worlds of academe and medicine, specialty shops with their colorful trappings and restaurants featuring the pungent flavors of the mysterious East may be found in almost every part of Chicago.

The adventure of Indian food is being enjoyed by more and more Chicagoans. The unusual dishes seasoned with unfamiliar spices and herbs present a new taste experience and challenge for intrepid Chicago cooks who are becoming knowledgeable in the use of coriander, cumin and cardamom.

Woman in traditional dress

CHAPATIS
(Bread)

Yield: 20 chapatis

3 cups all-purpose flour
1½ teaspoons salt
1 cup warm water

Save ½ cup flour for rolling dough. Mix remaining flour and salt in a large bowl. Add water, and mix to form a firm dough. Place in a lightly greased bowl, and cover with a tea towel. Let stand at least 1 hour (may stand overnight). Shape dough into 20 balls. Roll each ball into a thin flat circular shape, using reserved flour when necessary to keep dough from sticking. Allow chapatis to rest while heating a heavy, lightly oiled griddle to very hot. Cook bread 1 minute on each side, pressing gently around edges. Keep warm while cooking remaining chapatis. Serve with butter or very moist meat and vegetable dishes such as curries.

MULLIGATAWNY
(Soup)

Yield: 8 to 10 servings

2 pounds beef stew meat, cubed
2 pounds beef soup bones
1 teaspoon ground cardamom
3 cloves garlic
1½ teaspoons salt
2 tablespoons lemon juice
1 onion
4 whole cloves
1 tablespoon cumin seeds
1 tablespoon curry powder
10 peppercorns
1 tablespoon oil
3 onions, sliced
1 mustard seed
2 tablespoons curry powder
3 cups coconut milk

Into a large soup pot, place meat and bones and enough water to cover. Add cardamom, garlic, salt, lemon juice, onion studded with whole cloves, cumin seeds, curry powder and peppercorns. Cook over high heat until liquid begins to boil, then reduce heat to low and simmer 2 hours. When cool enough to handle, remove meat and discard bones. Reserve meat. Strain stock. Heat oil and fry onion until dark. Add mustard seed and curry powder and stir; add stock. Simmer gently for 10 minutes. Add coconut milk and meat. Heat gently.

HARAY DHANYA PATHA
(Coriander Leaf Salad)

Yield: 6 servings

chopped coriander leaves to serve 6 people (3 heads bibb lettuce may be substituted)

3 small onions, sliced
1½ tablespoons lemon juice
dash of salt

Lightly toss ingredients together; adjust salt if necessary. Chill covered until ready to serve.

The East Indian community celebrates Indian Independence Day in August. The program is rich with folklore, dances, folk music, speeches, and children's presentations. There are exhibits of Indian arts and crafts and various souvenirs that one may take home as mementoes. Patriotic songs and songs of the masses are sung, which share the philosophy of Rabindrinath Tagore, whose poetry has inspired the program's theme of universal brotherhood, peace and love. The programs are a most intriguing look at East Indian culture.

PATCHADI
(Indian Salad)

Yield: 4 servings

½ cup grated onion
1½ cups grated cucumber
1 large tomato, chopped
½ teaspoon salt
¼ teaspoon pepper
½ to ¾ cup yogurt

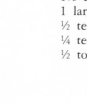

Mix onions, cucumber and tomato together. Season with salt and pepper. Add enough yogurt to coat mixture.

—Grace Mabbu Parthasarathy

TALAHOA SAZI
(Fried Vegetables)

Yield: 6 servings

1 teaspoon powdered mustard
1 tablespoon curry powder
dash chili powder
1½ teaspoons ground ginger
2 cloves garlic, crushed
1 teaspoon salt

3 tablespoons oil or melted butter
4 carrots, peeled and julienned
½ small cabbage, shredded
½ pound green beans, sliced
½ small cauliflower, sliced

Fry seasonings for a couple of minutes in hot oil or butter. Add vegetables. Cook, tossing gently until crisp, about 5 minutes. Adjust salt if necessary. Cover and cook a couple more minutes. Serve while hot.

TAAZI KHUMBEN ALU MATTARKARI
(Curried Vegetables)

Yield: 6 servings

1 onion, sliced
2 tablespoons melted butter
dash of ground ginger
dash of ground turmeric
1 clove garlic, crushed
dash of chili powder

1 pound small new potatoes,
  washed and quartered
8 ounces fresh or frozen peas
1 pound mushrooms, quartered
hot water

Fry onion gently in melted butter; add seasonings. Fry about 2 minutes. Add vegetables (if using frozen peas, do not add until last 10 minutes of cooking time). Add water (about ½ cup) and salt to taste. Cover and cook about 20 to 30 minutes until potatoes are tender.

ALOO-FRY
(Indian Style Potatoes)

Yield: 4 servings

½ cup onions, chopped
1½ tablespoons cooking oil
2 cups potatoes, peeled and diced

¼ cup chopped red pepper
½ teaspoon salt
1 cup water

Sauté onions in oil until lightly browned. Add potatoes, pepper, salt and water to cover scantly. Cover and steam cook over low heat for 20 to 25 minutes.

"Interesting women are in demand here" Quote from the New York *Star's* Chicago correspondent—1837

MASSALA GHOST
(Spiced Lamb)

Yield: 6 servings

2 pounds cubed lamb
2 small onions, chopped
2 teaspoons ground ginger
3 cloves garlic
½ cup cashews or almonds, chopped
4 dried chilies, seeded
1½ teaspoons ground cumin
2 teaspoons ground coriander

½ teaspoon each of following: ground cinnamon, ground cardamom, ground cloves
1 small onion, sliced
½ teaspoon saffron strands
2 tablespoons boiling water
2 tablespoons oil
2½ teaspoons salt
½ cup yogurt

Place chopped onion in blender with ginger, garlic, nuts, chilies and ½ cup water. Blend until smooth. Add remaining ground spices; and blend 1 minute. Soak saffron in 2 tablespoons boiling water while cooking onion-spice mixture. Fry sliced onion in hot oil until transparent. Add the blended mixture. Cook, stirring constantly, until oil begins to separate. Add ¼ cup water and salt; cook until water evaporates. Add lamb and stir to coat meat. Crush saffron and add to pan with yogurt; stir to blend. Cover and cook over low heat until meat is tender, about 1 hour, stirring occasionally. Serve over rice.

MURUG SALNA
(Chicken Curry)

Yield: 6 servings

3 tablespoons sunflower oil
2 large onions, chopped
3 cloves garlic, chopped
1 teaspoon grated fresh ginger
3 tablespoons curry powder
1 teaspoon chili powder, optional
2 teaspoons salt

3 ripe tomatoes, peeled and chopped
2 tablespoons chopped mint leaves
1 chicken (3½ pounds), cut into small serving pieces
½ cup yogurt
½ cup ground cashews, unsalted

Heat oil in large frying pan until hot. Reduce heat to medium. Slowly fry onion, garlic and ginger until onion is transparent. Stir occasionally with wooden spoon. Add next five ingredients; mix well. Add chicken, turning pieces to coat well with mixture. Cover and simmer until chicken is tender, about 45 minutes. Stir in yogurt and cashews. Heat thoroughly. Serve over cooked rice.

Note: Curry goes well with sieved hard-cooked egg yolk, cooked crumbled bacon, grated coconut and chopped cashews, served in small dishes from which diners may help themselves.

—A. Dhaliwal

MURUG
(Indian Chicken)

Yield: 4 servings

1 ⅓ cups onions, chopped fine
3 to 4 tablespoons cooking oil
4 chicken legs with thighs, skin removed
¼ teaspoon curry powder
¼ teaspoon ground coriander
½ teaspoon grated fresh ginger root
½ small clove garlic, minced
¼ teaspoon salt
¼ teaspoon pepper
3 tablespoons soy sauce
¼ cup water

Fry onion in hot oil until golden—use a large skillet so that chicken may be cooked in one layer. Place chicken over onion and sprinkle with seasonings. Pour soy sauce over chicken. Add enough water so that liquid covers the bottom of the pan. Turn chicken pieces to coat with sauce. Cover and cook over low heat for 15 minutes, stirring occasionally. Continue cooking, partially uncovered, for another 15 minutes, until chicken is tender. If there is too much liquid at the end, evaporate it somewhat by cooking for a few minutes uncovered. Serve over cooked rice.

GHOSH
(Indian Beef)

Yield: 4 servings

2 medium onions, chopped
1½ tablespoons cooking oil
1 pound beef, cut into slices about 4 inches in diameter and ¼-inch thick
½ teaspoon salt

¼ teaspoon pepper
½ teaspoon grated fresh ginger root
2 tablespoons Worcestershire sauce
1¼ cups water

Sauté onion in oil until golden. Add the beef slices and brown lightly on each side. Add salt, pepper and ginger. Pour the sauce over and add enough water to barely cover. Cover and cook, stirring occasionally, over low heat for about 40 minutes until beef is tender. Serve over rice or with Indian style potatoes.

PAYASAM
(Indian Dessert)

Yield: 6 servings

¼ cup white cashews
½ cup Indian vermicelli, cut into 1-inch lengths
¼ cup raisins
2 tablespoons butter
1 cup sweetened condensed milk
2 cups water
¼ teaspoon crushed cardamom

In saucepan, cook cashews, vermicelli and raisins in butter until butter foams up at edges. Add sweetened condensed milk and water gradually, stirring to blend. Bring to a boil and continue boiling until vermicelli becomes soft and expands, about 5 minutes. Spoon into sherbet glasses and sprinkle with cardamom.

RASMALAI
(Indian Dessert)

Yield: 6 servings

1½ cups ricotta cheese
1½ cups sugar

⅓ cup white cashews, sauteed in
    butter until golden
½ cup heavy cream

Preheat oven to 350 degrees F.

Mix cheese and sugar together. Put into 7-by-7-inch buttered baking dish and flatten mixture out to edges. Bake for 30 minutes. Sprinkle with cashews and pour cream over. Cut into squares.

KELA HALWA
(Banana Squares)

Yield: 2 dozen

6 medium ripe bananas, cut in
    small pieces
2 tablespoons melted butter

1 cup water
⅔ cup sugar
½ teaspoon ground cinnamon

Fry bananas in heavy skillet in melted butter until soft, about 5 minutes. Do not brown. Mash bananas; add water and sugar and blend well. Cook over medium heat until sugar melts and mixture is thick, about 20 minutes, stirring constantly. Remove from heat when mixture begins to come away from sides of pan. Add cinnamon; blend well. Pat into a shallow buttered dish. If butter begins to separate from mixture, pour it off. When cool, cut into squares.

Although plain rice is the common accompaniment of most East Indian main dishes, here is a colorful variation. After cooking 1 cup rice in the unusal manner, add ½ cup minced onions which have been sautéed in butter, and ¼ cup each cooked diced carrots and peas.

The English, Scots and Welsh

One of the earliest believers in Chicago was John Kinzie, a Canadian-born Scot who came to the settlement in 1804. His lucrative trading activities with the Indians were briefly interrupted by the total destruction of the infant Fort Dearborn and the resultant dispersion of both the military and civilian population. Undaunted by the setback, Kinzie returned a few years later to resume and expand his business enterprises, and in 1833 he became the first president of the village of Chicago. The Kinzie House, spacious and well appointed for its time, according to the descriptions of visitors, was located at the mouth of the Chicago River. The lot on which it rested now forms the base of a skyscraper overlooking the lake and the river at 400 North Michigan Avenue.

Another illustrious early Chicagoan was Captain John Whistler who commanded the ill-fated first Fort Dearborn. The Captain was an Irish-born British subject when he served under General Burgoyne in the Revolutionary War. He later became the grandfather of the great American painter, James McNeill Whistler.

One of the more colorful members of those early settlers from the British Isles was Billy Caldwell. Of British and Indian parentage, Caldwell, or Sauganash as the Indians called him, was active in Indian affairs as well as those concerning the European settlers of the little village.

As the city grew, more and more expatriates from the islands in the North Atlantic came to the shores of Lake Michigan. By 1860 there were almost 4,400 Chicagoans of English origin, over 1,640 with Scottish ancestry, and over two hundred from the ancient Celtic country of Wales. Although a small Scottish community existed for many years in the Lincoln Park area, most of the members of this immigrant group moved with little difficulty into the mainstream of city life, making their contributions to the business, social and political aspects of Chicago's development. By 1900 there were over 102,000 foreign-born and first generation Americans from England, Scotland and Wales.

The cuisine from the British Isles formed many of the early food and menu patterns of Chicago. Hearty breads, unadorned fish and meat dishes and toothsome desserts are but a part of that cooking legacy which Chicago enjoys.

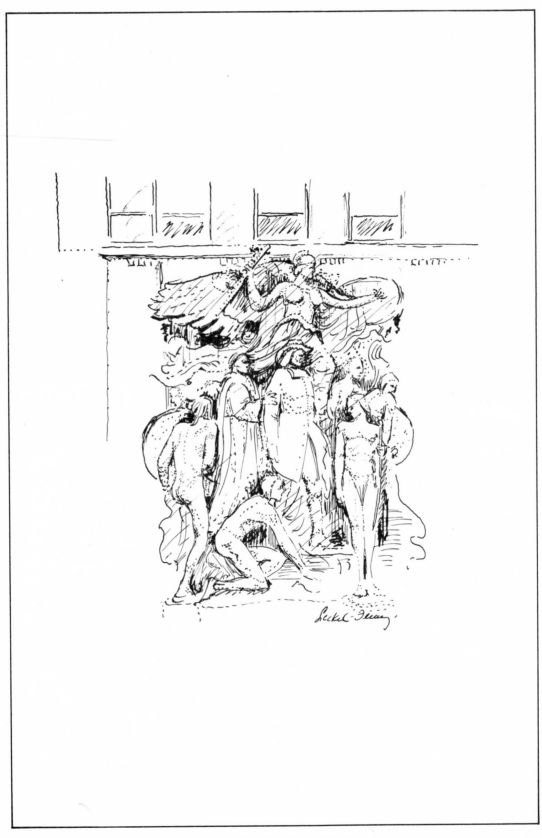

Relief sculpture, The Explorers, *on the north pylon of the Michigan Avenue Bridge close to the site of the John Kinzie House*

DRIED FRUIT TEA LOAF

Yield: 1 loaf

¾ cup dried apricots
¾ cup dried prunes
¼ cup (½ stick) butter
1 cup light corn syrup
2 cups flour

3 teaspoons baking powder
¼ teaspoon salt
1 egg, beaten
½ cup milk

Preheat oven to 400 degrees F.

Cover fruit with cold water and soak for one-half hour. Drain and cut into small pieces. Cream together butter and corn syrup. Add 1/3 of sifted dry ingredients. Beat in egg and blend thoroughly. Add remaining dry ingredients alternately with milk; fold in dried fruit. Pour into buttered 9-by-5-by-3-inch loaf pan and bake for 45 minutes until top crust is golden.

—*Agnes Whalen*

COCKALEEKIE SOUP

Yield: 6 to 8 servings

1 stewing hen
2½ quarts water
2 tablespoons chopped parsley

salt and pepper
10 leeks, chopped
10 pitted prunes

Stew the hen for 1½ hours in water with the parsley, salt, pepper and 3 of the leeks. Remove the hen. Strain the broth and return broth to kettle. Add the remaining leeks and simmer for 15 minutes. Add the cut up white meat of the hen and the prunes; simmer an additional 15 minutes. Serve hot.

—*Jane Kutza*

"The town that Billy Sunday could not shut down"

LEEKS AND POTATOES IN CHEESE SAUCE

Yield: 6 to 8 servings

5 large potatoes, peeled and sliced
    thin
6 leeks, sliced
2½ tablespoons flour
⅓ cup butter
2 cups milk, generous
salt and pepper
⅛ teaspoon mace
¼ cup sharp cheese, grated

Preheat oven to 350 degrees F.
Layer the potatoes and leeks in a 2-quart casserole dish. Make a roux of the flour and butter. Add the milk, salt, pepper and mace and simmer until thick. Add the cheese and pour over potatoes and leeks. Bake for 50 minutes covered. Remove cover and bake 20 minutes longer until bubbly and browned.

SHEPHERD'S PIE

Yield: 4 servings

5 cups mashed potatoes
2 eggs, beaten
2 tablespoons melted butter
1 pound leftover roast
1 large onion, chopped
salt and pepper
leftover gravy
1 egg yolk
1 tablespoon water

Preheat oven to 350 degrees F.
Mix mashed potatoes with 2 beaten eggs and butter. Line a 9-inch pie tin with half of the potato mixture. Slice the meat thin and place over potatoes. Sprinkle on onions, salt, pepper and any leftover gravy; cover with a layer of mashed potatoes. Paint with yolk mixed with water. Bake until browned.

—Marge Bonelli

BOILED BEEF BRISKET WITH BAKING POWDER DUMPLINGS

Yield: 6 servings

5 pound beef brisket
1 tablespoon butter
1 teaspoon cooking oil
1 small soup bone
12 carrots, scraped and cut into
     3-inch chunks
2 onions, quartered
½ teaspoon thyme
1 bay leaf
1 teaspoon parsley flakes
1 teaspoon salt
½ teaspoon pepper
2 tablespoons horseradish mixed
     with ½ cup heavy cream

In a large pot brown the brisket on all sides in the butter and oil. Add soup bone, 2 carrots, onions and seasonings and add water to cover. When mixture boils, reduce heat, cover and simmer for about 2 hours. Add remaining carrots and check seasonings. Let cook for another 35 minutes, until carrots are tender. Place dumplings on top of mixture a tablespoonful at a time. Cover and cook for 12 minutes until dumplings are light and fluffy. Add a dollop of horseradish mixture to each serving.

Dumplings

1 cup flour
1⅓ teaspoons baking powder
½ teaspoon salt

1 tablespoon butter
½ cup milk

Sift dry ingredients together. Cut in butter. Add milk and mix lightly.

—Fred Bremer

In 1860, Chicago Mayor "Long John" Wentworth was asked how it felt to sit next to the future King of England. Long John answered, "I was not sitting beside the Prince. He sat beside me."

FORFAR BRIDIES

Yield: 10 servings

2½ cups twice-sifted flour
1 teaspoon salt
¾ cup butter
cold water
1½ pounds ground round steak
3 tablespoons suet, chopped fine
1 onion, diced small
¼ teaspoon mace
salt and pepper
1 egg
2 tablespoons water

Preheat oven to 375 degrees F.

Sift together flour and salt. Cut in the butter until pea-sized lumps are formed. Add enough water to hold together. Chill for 15 minutes, then roll out and cut into 10 5-inch circles. Mix the meat, suet and seasonings together thoroughly. Divide the meat mixture onto the 10 pastry circles. Fold each over and pinch together, sealing with a little water. Beat the egg and water together and paint the tops of the bridies with it. Prick the tops to let steam escape. Place on a rack on a cookie sheet and bake 35 to 40 minutes until golden. Serve warm.

—*T. M. McKinley*

The annual Feast of the Haggis is held during the first week of December by Chicago Scots. This formal event is sponsored by the St. Andrew's Society and is held in a hotel dining room for the benefit of the Scottish home. A queen is chosen, bagpipes perform, and a sumptuous dinner of meat pies, sausage rolls, short bread and Haggis is served. The Haggis is a Scots type of dressing which is made from sheep innards mixed fine with onions, suet and oatmeal and packed in the sheep's stomach and boiled.

DEVILED KIDNEYS

Yield: 4 servings

10 lamb kidneys, skinned and cored
¼ cup butter
2 tablespoons Dijon-type mustard

1 tablespoon Worcestershire sauce
salt and pepper
8 toast triangles

Slice the kidneys and sauté them in butter until cooked through. Mix the mustard, sauce, salt and pepper. Swirl into the kidneys. Cover and cook over medium-low heat for 2 minutes. Serve over toast.

LANCASHIRE HOT POT

Yield: 6 servings

5 large potatoes, peeled and sliced
1½ pounds lamb, cubed small
3 lamb kidneys, cubed
2 medium onions, chopped

salt and pepper
1 cup water
4 tablespoons (½ stick) butter
parsley

Preheat oven to 350 degrees F.

Line the bottom of a 2-quart casserole dish with a thick layer of potatoes; place the cubed meat on the potatoes. Cover the meat with the onions, salt and pepper and water. Layer the rest of the potatoes into the casserole. Dot with butter and bake for 2 hours. Garnish each serving with parsley.

—John Ewing

When visiting Chicago, Oscar Wilde was amazed that "such good wine could be obtained so far west."

TRIFLE

Yield: 8 servings

1 9-inch sponge cake, stale	2 tablespoons lemon juice
5 tablespoons sherry	1 teaspoon grated lemon rind
4 egg yolks	1 cup whipping cream, whipped
½ cup sugar	2 tablespoons sugar
⅛ teaspoon salt	1 teaspoon vanilla
2½ cups milk, scalded	almond halves
1 teaspoon vanilla	candied cherry halves

Break cake into 1-inch cubes; sprinkle with sherry. In a double boiler, mix together egg yolks, ½ cup sugar and salt. Stir in hot milk slowly. Cook until custard coats a metal spoon. Add vanilla, lemon juice and rind. Chill. Cover bottom of 2-quart tube mold with 1/3 of cake cubes. Cover with 1/3 of custard. Repeat until used. Cover, then chill overnight. Unmold. Garnish with whipped cream flavored with sugar and vanilla. Decorate with almond and cherry halves.

—Lockwood Wiley

LACE OATMEAL COOKIES

Yield: 4 dozen

1 cup (2 sticks) softened butter	1 cup flour
½ cup sugar	½ teaspoon salt
1 cup brown sugar (packed firmly)	½ teaspoon baking soda
1 egg	2¾ cups uncooked oatmeal
1½ teaspoons vanilla	1¼ cups quartered pecans

Preheat oven to 350 degrees F.

Cream butter with brown and granulated sugars until light and airy. Add egg and vanilla and beat until smooth. Sift flour, salt and baking soda together and gradually beat into butter mixture, blending well. Add oatmeal and nuts and blend thoroughly. Place 1-inch diameter balls of cookie dough about 2 inches apart on cookie sheet covered with foil. Bake for 12 to 15 minutes until cookies have browned and spread. Let cool for 5 minutes and remove from cookie sheet with a spatula.

—Judy Solomon

LEMON MERINGUE PIE

Yield: 8 servings

Dough

1½ cups flour
½ cup butter
1 teaspoon salt
3 tablespoons water

Preheat oven to 400 degrees F.

Mix ingredients together with a fork. Gather dough together and roll out. Place loosely in a 9-inch, deep dish pie tin and prick here and there with a fork. Pinch edges of crust with thumb and forefinger to create a raised ridge around pie crust. Bake for 20 to 25 minutes until golden brown. Cool.

Lemon Filling

3 cups sugar
⅔ cup cornstarch
3 cups very hot water
6 egg yolks, lightly beaten

5 tablespoons butter
juice and grated rind of 2 large lemons

Sift sugar and cornstarch together in large saucepan. Add hot water gradually, stirring to blend thoroughly. Place over medium heat and bring to a boil, stirring continuously. Drop about 3 tablespoons of the hot mixture into beaten egg yolks and blend. Add egg yolk mixture to boiling mixture in saucepan and continue boiling for about one minute, stirring constantly. Remove from heat and blend in butter, lemon juice and grated lemon rind. Mix thoroughly until blended and smooth. Pour into cooled pie crust shell and allow to cool.

Meringue

6 egg whites
½ teaspoon cream of tartar
⅔ cup sugar

Preheat oven to 400 degrees F.

Beat cream of tartar and egg whites together until the mixture is foamy. Gradually add sugar and continue beating until stiff peaks are formed. Mound meringue onto cooled lemon filling in pie crust shell, making sure that meringue seals edges of pastry. Place in middle rack of oven until evenly browned and set, about 10 to 12 minutes.

—T. M. McCann

The French

French explorers were the first Europeans to discover the Chicago area and its Portage. Even before it became a city, the little settlement on the lake included a number of French-speaking inhabitants. Two of the more colorful Gallic members of the community were the Beaubien brothers, who had come to Chicago to seek a living amid the Indian residents and the handful of settlers clustered around Fort Dearborn. Mark Beaubien's hotel, The Sauganash Inn, was erected at Pine (Michigan) Avenue and Randolph Street, a site near one that is now occupied by the Chicago Public Library. The hotel became a legend in its own time, featuring good food and spirits with music and entertainment often provided by Mark Beaubien himself.

It was through the efforts of the early French population that the first mission from the St. Louis diocese was established in Chicago. A priest was sent to the new mission, and in 1833 Chicago's first church, St. Mary's, was built at the corner of Lake and State Streets., Built of wood, the little church housed the French worshippers as well as their Catholic counterparts from Germany and Ireland who soon outnumbered them. Because of its cultural and historic significance, its loss in the 1871 Great Fire was tragic.

The French community grew with the arrival of immigrants from France and Canada and spread to the south of the city's center, building its own church there in the mid-nineteenth century. Although this building was also destroyed in the Great Fire, Notre Dame Church, built near Racine and Harrison Streets in 1864, is a reminder of the early French heritage of the city.

Several other French communities were begun on the far south side as population shifts took place, and by 1900, besides the many third and fourth generation French and French Canadians living in the city, there were 9,000 foreign-born and their children who had adopted Chicago as their own.

Much of the world is familiar with the haute cuisine of France, but the cooking which developed in the kitchens of French Chicagoans bears more resemblance to French Canadian and provincial French cuisines than that which was refined and developed in the sophisticated bistros of the City of Light. Using the produce at hand, but with an unmistakable French flair, these recipes represent food preparation raised to an art form.

Notre Dame Church, 1335 W. Harrison

PAIN AUX DATTES ET AUX NOIX
(Date and Nut Bread)

Yield: 1 loaf

1¼ teaspoons baking soda
1 cup boiling water
1 package pitted dates, chopped
1½ cups flour
½ teaspoon salt
2 tablespoons butter
1 cup granulated sugar
1 egg
1½ teaspoons vanilla
½ cup chopped pecans or walnuts

Preheat oven to 350 degrees F.

Dissolve baking soda in boiling water and pour water over dates. Set aside until cool. Sift flour and salt together. In a mixing bowl, cream butter and sugar. Beat in egg and vanilla and add flour mixture. Fold in dates and chopped nuts. Bake in buttered loaf pan for 40 minutes.

—Mary Dalzell

POTAGE AU POISSON
(Fish Soup)

Yield: 8 servings

2 large potatoes, peeled and cubed
1½ cups celery, chopped
1 carrot, sliced
2 onions, minced
3½ pounds haddock, skinned,
    boned and cut into 1-inch pieces
2 bay leaves

½ teaspoon savory
1½ teaspoons salt
½ teaspoon pepper
2 tablespoons butter
2½ tablespoons flour
3 cups cream, hot but not boiling
1 tablespoon parsley flakes

Place potatoes, celery, carrot, onions, fish, bay leaves and other seasonings in large saucepan. Cover with water and cook over medium high heat for about 25 minutes. Remove from heat. Make a roux of the butter and flour. Remove from heat and gradually add cream, stirring until blended and thick. Add to the fish mixture, blending thoroughly. Taste for seasoning. If soup is too thick, a little milk may be added. Sprinkle with parsley flakes.

AVOCATS AVEC LA SAUCE DOUCE
(Avocados with Sweet Dressing)

Yield: 6 servings

⅓ cup raisins
2 cups cottage cheese or ricotta
1½ tablespoons olive oil
juice of one lemon
juice of one orange

salt and pepper
6 large lettuce leaves
6 avocados
fresh mint
thin strips of orange rind

Dressing

Puree raisins in blender or food processor. Add cheese and blend until smooth. Beat in olive oil and juices. Add salt and pepper to taste. Chill.

Wash and drain lettuce leaves. Arrange one each on salad plates. Peel and pit avocados and slice in half. Arrange on lettuce leaves. Generously spoon dressing over avocados. Garnish with mint leaves and orange strips.

Mark Beaubien, owner of the Sauganash Hotel, was accused of owning only two blankets. As soon as the most recent guests fell asleep, he removed their blankets and gave them to the next two registering guests.

SAUCE AUX HARICOTS VERTS
(Green Beans in White Sauce)

Yield: 6 servings

2 medium onions, chopped
3 tablespoons butter
3½ tablespoons flour
2½ cups light cream, hot but not boiling
1 teaspoon salt

½ teaspoon pepper
½ teaspoon nutmeg
1½ pounds cooked green beans
4 hard-cooked eggs, sliced in thick rounds

In a large saucepan sauté onions in butter until transparent. Add flour and make roux. Remove pan from heat and slowly add hot cream, stirring until thick and smooth. Bring to a boil slowly and add salt, pepper and nutmeg. Add green beans and hard-cooked eggs. Blend thoroughly.

—Roberta Michaletz

SAUCISSE FOURRE
(Baked Sausage)

Yield: 6 servings

1 ½-pound chunk of Swiss cheese
12 strips of bacon
6 serving size smoked sausages (Polish or Italian sausage may be used if they are divided in half)

Dijon-type mustard
12 toothpicks

Preheat oven to 400 degrees F.

Cut Swiss cheese into 6 long strips about ⅛ inch wide; coat each with mustard. Remove skin from sausages. Make a slit lengthwise in sausage. Place cheese strips in slits in sausage. Wrap 2 bacon strips around each sausage, securing each with a toothpick. Bake for about 25 to 30 minutes or until bacon is crisp and cheese is bubbly.

TOURTIERE
(Meat Pie)

Yield: 6 servings

1½ pounds ground pork, fat
  removed
1 garlic clove, crushed
2 onions, minced
¼ teaspoon cloves, ground
½ teaspoon thyme, dried
1 teaspoon salt
½ teaspoon pepper
2 small bay leaves
scant half cup boiling water
pastry dough for 8-inch two crust
  pie
1 egg beaten with 1 tablespoon
  water

Preheat oven to 375 degrees F.

Mix pork with garlic, onions, cloves, thyme, salt, pepper and bay leaves. Place in large skillet and pour boiling water over. Simmer for about 25 minutes. Pour off grease and discard bay leaves. Pour mixture into uncooked pie shell; cover with top crust. Make a hole about ½ inch in diameter in center of top crust. Brush top with egg and water mixture. Bake for 40 minutes, until pie is nicely browned.

—*Berenice Gareau*

Chicago francophiles have revived the time-honored celebration of Bastille Day. There is a street dance, and bands; mimes and choirs perform. Accordionists stroll about playing while astrologists and palmists intimate the future. "The Marseillaise" is sung and French restaurants on East Ontario Street provide special menus at special prices. Champagne is served.

The "make no small plans" city

BOEUF À LA PAYSANNE
(Beef Stew)

Yield: 6 servings

3 pounds beef stew meat cut into
    2-inch cubes
¾ teaspoon thyme, dried
1 bay leaf
½ teaspoon rosemary, dried
4 onions, chopped
8 carrots, scraped and sliced
½ teaspoon black pepper
1½ teaspoons salt
3 cups light, dry red wine

2 tablespoons cooking oil
2 tablespoons butter
2 garlic cloves, crushed
flour
1 pound fresh green beans, washed,
    trimmed, and left whole
6 turnips, peeled and cut into
    1-inch cubes
2 tablespoons very heavy cream

Put beef in deep earthenware bowl. Add thyme, bay leaf, rosemary, ½ of the onions, about ¼ of the carrots, pepper, salt and wine. Cover bowl with foil, and occasionally turn meat pieces. Let marinate for 6 to 8 hours (or overnight). Strain marinade, reserving liquid; drain meat on paper towels. Place oil and butter in large saucepan over moderate heat. Add meat, the rest of the chopped onions, and the crushed garlic. When nicely browned, skim off excess grease and sprinkle flour over meat mixture, stirring well to blend. Carefully stir in marinade mixture and taste for correct seasoning. Cover and cook for 1 hour over medium low heat. Meanwhile, cook green beans for 15 minutes in lightly salted boiling water. After meat has cooked 1 hour, add carrots to meat and cook for an additional 15 minutes. Add green beans, turnips and mushrooms and cook for 15 minutes more. Remove meat to warm platter, and spoon out vegetables to surround it. Keep platter warm. If the stew liquid is too thin, boil rapidly over high heat to reduce it in volume. Swirl in cream and remove from heat. Pour the sauce over the meat and serve very hot.

Chicago hostesses, expecting distinguished visitors from New York for the Columbian Exposition, were warned by an Eastern advisor in social etiquette not to "frappé their wine too much."

GALANTINE DE POULET
(Chicken in Aspic)

Yield: 8 servings

2 3-pound frying chickens
½ teaspoon salt, divided
2 teaspoons dried tarragon, divided
2 shallots, minced, green tops
　　and all
1 tablespoon butter
1 teaspoon cooking oil
1 stalk of celery, finely chopped
1 carrot, finely chopped
1 large onion, finely chopped
1 bay leaf
2 sprigs of fresh thyme
1½ teaspoons dried parsley
1½ teaspoons salt
1 teaspoon pepper
1 cup dry white wine

Wash the chickens and dry inside and out. Rub inside of each chicken with ¼ teaspoon salt and 1 teaspoon dried tarragon. Place minced shallots inside cavity. In a large kettle brown chicken in melted butter and oil. Add about 2 quarts of water and all other ingredients. Bring to a boil over high heat. Lower heat, cover kettle and let simmer for about 1 hour until chicken is tender. Remove chicken from liquid and boil the stock until reduced by half in volume. Bone chicken and cut into bite-sized pieces. Place chicken in oiled gelatin mold and pour the liquid on top. Refrigerate overnight. Unmold when ready to serve and garnish with greens or cherry tomatoes.

TARTE AU SUCRE
(Sugar Pie)

Yield: 6 to 8 servings

4¾ cups light maple syrup
1¾ cups very heavy cream
¾ cup chopped walnuts and hazel-
　　nuts, mixed

Put the maple syrup in a saucepan and reduce it by 1/3 over medium heat. Add the cream and let the mixture cook, stirring constantly, until it reaches the consistency of light cream. Remove from heat, fold in the chopped nuts and let cool. Preheat oven to 375 degrees F.

Crust

2 tablespoons sugar
½ teaspoon baking powder
pinch of salt
2 cups flour

⅓ cup butter
⅓ cup shortening
1 egg
2 teaspoons melted butter

Sift dry ingredients together. Cut in butter and shortening. Add egg, mixing thoroughly. A few drops of water may be added if paste is too dry. Roll out on lightly floured surface and fit into 8-inch pie plan, fluting edges with fork. Drizzle melted butter over surface. Pour filling into uncooked pie shell. Bake for 40 to 45 minutes.

BEIGNETS AUX POMMES
(Apple Fritters)

Yield: 6 servings

2 cups plus 2 tablespoons flour
½ teaspoon salt
1½ tablespoons baking powder
2 tablespoons brown sugar
6 tablespoons granulated sugar
½ teaspoon mace
1 teaspoon cinnamon
2 eggs
1 tablespoon cream
1 cup milk
3 large apples
½ cup cooking oil

Sift flour, salt and baking powder together and set aside. Mix sugars and spices together. Beat eggs with 1 tablespoon of cream and add sugar mixture, blending thoroughly. Alternately add flour mixture and milk, mixing thoroughly. Peel and slice apples. Coat apple slices in dough and fry in hot oil until browned (370 degrees F.). Drain on paper towels and sprinkle with powdered sugar.

Every family in early Chicago kept a cow for a fresh milk supply. A single cowherd was hired by all to collect the cattle each morning and take them to pasture on the outskirts of the city. The evening saw him prodding them along, udders full, to the homes of their owners to be relieved of their precious burden for the evening meal.

The Germans

German immigrants originally came to Chicago attracted by the potential employment available on the Illinois-Michigan Canal. Within a few years after the gala ground breaking ceremonies on July 4, 1836, their numbers came to about 700. They settled just north of the South Branch of the Chicago River. Churches of various denominations were established by the early German-speaking population at LaSalle and Ohio Streets, between Wells and Franklin Streets at Washington Street, and at Chicago and Wabash Avenues.

Another manifestation of their culture was reflected in the establishment of the first brewery in Chicago in 1839, at Chicago and Pine (Michigan) Avenues. Several beer gardens flourished in the section near the center of the city where there was a concentration of German immigrants. The German Beer Riots occurred in 1855 because of Sunday "blue laws," and as a consequence the Sunday closings were rescinded.

As the city grew, other German communities sprang up north and south of the Chicago River and in some of the unincorporated outlying farm areas. As their numbers grew, so did their influence in the political, industrial, cultural and religious aspects of the developing city. By 1870 the German population numbered over 52,000 and in 1950 there were over a quarter of a million Germans of foreign stock in Chicago.

German food is rarely light. It has a robustness which in no way resembles the frivolousness of some of the lighter cuisines. The meats and produce supplied by the farmers in the outlying areas were well suited to the German taste. Pork and fowl were plentiful and both found their way into many German dishes. These dishes are typical of the German-American fare found in Chicago today.

St. Michael's Church in Old Town

ZWIEBELKUCHEN
(Onion Cake)

Yield: 8 to 10 servings

Crust

6 tablespoons bacon fat
1 cup plus 6 tablespoons flour
salt
⅓ cup milk
1 teaspoon baking powder

Cream fat. Add all other ingredients in order given. Knead and roll out to size of a large cookie sheet; place on cookie sheet or in a 13-by-9-by-2-inch baking pan. Pull up sides of dough to form a rim.

Filling

8 large onions, chopped
3 tablespoons butter
6 tablespoons flour
1⅓ cups sour cream or sour milk

2 to 4 eggs
salt (1 to 2 teaspoons)
caraway seeds (1 to 2 teaspoons)
5 bacon slices

Preheat oven to 375 degrees F.

Cook onions in butter until shiny; cool before adding to remaining ingredients. Blend flour and sour cream, eggs, salt, caraway seeds together. Add cooled onions to this mixture and spread over pastry Crust. Cross with bacon strips. Bake for 45 minutes to 1 hour.

"I wish I could go to America if only to see that Chicago." Quote from Otto von Bismark, Imperial Chancellor of Germany, 1870.

ALLERLEI
(Mixed Vegetables)

Yield: 6 to 8 servings

3 carrots, cut in 2-inch lengths
1 large kohlrabi, sliced
¼ pound string beans
8 asparagus spears, cut in 2-inch
   lengths
½ small head cauliflower

½ pound mushrooms
2 tablespoons flour
½ cup butter
1 cup vegetable water
salt and pepper

Wash and prepare the vegetables. Place them in a pot of boiling water in order given, according to the amount of time each takes to cook. The mushrooms will require only 1 minute. Drain the vegetables carefully, reserving 1 cup of liquid. Make a roux of the flour and butter. Add enough vegetable water to make a thick sauce. Season with salt and pepper; return the vegetables to the sauce and bring up to a simmer. Serve.

SPAETZEL
(Egg Dumplings)

Yield: 6 servings

2 eggs
½ cup water
1½ cups flour

½ teaspoon salt
¼ teaspoon baking powder

Beat eggs and water and add to the dry ingredients. Drop by teaspoon into boiling water, or drip through a coarse colander. Spaetzel should be light and fluffy. If too heavy, add more water to batter. Simmer until done. Drain and keep warm. Sauté ¼ cup bread crumbs in ½ cup butter. Pour over Spaetzel.

NUDELN
(Noodles)

Yield: 6 to 8 servings

3 eggs
1 teaspoon salt
2 cups flour
¼ cup melted butter

Beat eggs and salt together until frothy. Sift in flour. Mix. Knead, roll thin (1/16 inch), and brush with butter. Slice diagonally in ¾-inch strips and roll each noodle up. Drop in boiling soup and cook for about 15 minutes.

EIER MIT ROSINEN SCHMARRN
(Egg Puff with Raisins)

Yield: 6 servings

6 tablespoons white raisins
6 eggs
3¼ teaspoons sugar
1 cup 2 tablespoons milk
1½ cups twice-sifted flour
pinch of salt
butter
confectioner's sugar

Soak raisins in water to cover for one hour; pat dry. Separate the eggs. Combine yolks with sugar, milk, flour and salt and blend well. Fold stiffly beaten egg whites and raisins into egg mixture gently. Melt butter in a skillet and fry the Schmarrn in 1/5 portions on each side. Do not overfry. Take each from pan, pull apart with a fork into bite-size pieces, sprinkle with confectioner's sugar. When all are done, return pieces to the pan and fry gently in butter. Place on serving dish and sprinkle with confectioner's sugar.

BIER-SCHMORBRAD
(Beer Stew)

Yield: 6 to 8 servings

3 pounds beef stew meat, cut into
    ½-inch cubes
flour
butter
16 ounces beer
¾ cup water

1 tablespoon brown sugar
3 very large onions, sliced
salt and pepper
10 whole cloves
4 tablespoons flour
water

Dredge meat in flour. Brown in butter in a large pot with a tight-fitting lid. Add beer, water and brown sugar. Cover and simmer about 2 hours. ¾ hour before meat is tender, add onions, salt, pepper and cloves. Thicken, if necessary, with a paste of flour and water. May be served with dumplings.

—*F. Thurlow Meyer*

SAUERBRATEN MIT PFEFFERKUCHEN
(Sauerbraten with Gingersnaps)

Yield: 6 to 8 servings

1 4- to 5-pound beef round, rump
    or chuck
3 teaspoons salt
2½ cups red wine
1 cup water
1½ cups sliced onion
¾ cup sliced carrot
½ cup sliced celery
6 whole peppercorns

5 whole cloves
2 bay leaves
2 tablespoons cooking oil
¼ cup firmly packed brown sugar
¼ cup flour
½ cup water
½ teaspoon salt
12 gingersnaps, crushed

Place meat in large bowl; sprinkle with salt. Combine wine, 1 cup water, vegetables, spices and herbs in a saucepan; bring to boil. Pour over meat. Cover meat and refrigerate for 24 hours. Remove meat from marinade. Dry. Brown meat well on both sides in hot oil. Sprinkle with brown sugar. Strain marinade. Add vegetables and spices to meat. Pour 1 cup marinade over meat. Cover: cook meat very slowly until tender, about 3 hours. Remove meat from pan and slice. Keep warm. Strain liquid; skim off fat. Add marinade to pan liquid as needed to make 3 cups. Blend together flour, ½ cup water and ½ teaspoon salt. Add to liquid in pan; cook, stirring constantly, until thickened and smooth. Stir in gingersnaps; heat. Serve over sliced meat.

LEBER MIT APFELN UND ZWIEBELN
(Liver with Apples and Onions)

Yield: 4 servings

1½ pounds of calves' liver
cracker crumbs
salt and pepper
3 tablespoons butter
3 cups sliced onions
4 apples, peeled, cored and sliced
2 tablespoons brown sugar
juice of ½ lemon

Cut liver into serving size pieces. Coat with the crumbs, season with salt and pepper, and saute in butter until browned but still pink inside. Remove and keep warm. Sauté onions in butter until soft; remove and keep warm. Sprinkle apple slices with sugar and lemon juice, then sauté in butter until golden. Arrange apples and onions on liver; serve.

—Mary Zeckler

"City of the broad shoulders"

KRINGLES

Yield: 4 dozen

2 cups twice-sifted flour, divided
dash of salt
2 teaspoons baking powder
1 cup granulated sugar
½ cup softened unsalted butter

1 egg, beaten
½ tablespoon caraway seeds
3½ tablespoons brandy
½ cup confectioner's sugar

Preheat oven to 375 degrees F.

Sift together 1½ cups flour, salt and baking powder. In a separate bowl, cream suger and butter. Beat in the egg, caraway seeds and brandy. Add flour mixture. Add more flour if needed to make dough stiff enough to handle. Roll ⅛ inch thick. Cut in crescent shapes. Sprinkle with confectioner's sugar. Bake for 12 minutes.

PFEFFERKUCHEN
(Ginger Cookies)

Yield: 5 dozen

1¼ cups sugar
3 eggs
3 cups flour

1½ tablespoons ginger
1½ tablespoons grated lemon rind

Beat sugar and eggs together, blending thoroughly. Sift flour with ginger and gradually add flour to sugar. Stir in grated lemon rind. When dough is thoroughly blended, divide into two sections. Roll each out on lightly floured surface to about ⅛ inch thickness. Cut into circles about 2 inches in diameter with drinking glass and place about 1 inch apart on cookie sheet which has been lined with foil. Let stand 45 minutes before placing in oven. Preheat oven to 325 degrees F. Bake for 12 minutes until golden. Remove to flat surface with spatula.

PLUM KUCHEN
(Plum Cake)

Yield: 2 cakes

½ cup softened butter
¼ cup sugar
¼ teaspoon mace
¾ teaspoon salt
1 cup scalded milk
2 eggs, beaten
1 cake compressed yeast
2 tablespoons sugar
4 cups sifted flour

Mix together butter, sugar, mace and salt; pour hot milk over. When cooled to lukewarm, stir in beaten eggs, then yeast which has been softened with 2 tablespoons sugar, and add enough flour to make a soft dough. Mix with a spoon, then turn onto a floured board and knead until smooth. Shape into a ball. Place in buttered bowl and brush with melted butter; cover with towel and let rise in a warm place until doubled, about 1 hour. Divide dough and shape each part into a ball. Pat and roll each to fit a 10-inch round or square pan which has been well buttered. Pull and stretch dough to make it come up about 1 inch on all sides.

Topping

2 tablespoons softened butter
6 tablespoons graham cracker
  crumbs
20 purple plums, quartered
1 cup sugar

1 teaspoon cinnamon
2 egg yolks
2 tablespoons heavy cream
¼ cup melted butter

Spread each cake with softened butter, then with graham cracker crumbs. Let stand 15 minutes. Lay quartered plums in parallel rings on top of crumbs. Mix sugar and cinnamon together. Lightly beat together egg yolks, cream and melted butter. Sprinkle plums on each cake with half the sugar and cinnamon topping, and then half the egg mixture. Let stand 20 minutes. Preheat oven to 350 degrees F. Bake for 50 minutes.

—*Mildred Sawusch*

KIRSCHKUCHEN
(Cherry Cake)

Yield: 1 cake

2 eggs
3 tablespoons butter
¾ cup sugar
1½ cups twice-sifted flour
¼ teaspoon salt

2¾ teaspoons baking powder
½ cup cream
1 teaspoon vanilla
2 cups pitted fresh cherries

Preheat oven to 375 degrees F.

Separate the eggs. Cream together butter, sugar, and well-beaten egg yolks. Add flour, salt and baking powder. Add cream gradually, beating constantly. Add vanilla and fold in stiffly beaten egg whites. Butter and flour a tube pan. Place cherries on bottom and spoon batter over them, pressing it down gently. Bake for 35 minutes or until done. Remove from pan.

The flood of immigrants that came to Chicago with the opening of the Erie Canal in 1835 occasioned a price ceiling law to protect them from overly eager purveyors: 12½¢ for a pint of whiskey, 25¢ for a pint of brandy or rum, 25¢ for dinner or breakfast, and 12½¢ for lodgings.

German Day is held in Buffalo Grove in the middle of July. The festival is patterned after a giant picnic, with ethnic German foods served including bratwurst, thuringer and German potato salad. Participants sit under a large tent listening to speakers from the German Consulate and other visiting dignitaries. Beer and coffee are served with delicious German pastries. Folk dancing and various kinds of German music highlight the festivities.

The Greeks

Only a few Greeks were known to have lived in Chicago before the Great Fire. After the conflagration, a group of Greek men came to the city to explore the opportunities presented in the reconstruction work. Two tiny Greek communities were in existence in Pullman and on the west side before the political strife in their Mediterranean homeland caused a mass migration to this country in the 1890s.

The early development of self-help groups and fraternal organizations characterized the will of Greek immigrants to perpetuate their nationalistic heritage. A church was organized in temporary quarters and national language schools were established. It wasn't until the late 1890s that the first Greek Orthodox Church was finally established in the "Delta," the triangle formed by Blue Island Avenue and Harrison and Halsted Streets.

Fruit and vegetable markets, sweet shops, restaurants and flower shops were but a few of the small businesses initiated by these new but eager Chicagoans. With education as a top priority, many of the sons and daughters of the first wave of Greek immigrants were able to enter professions such as law and medicine, further adding to the city's vitality.

The Greek community numbered about 15,600 by the year 1920. Newer communities had settled on the north side, the south side and later in South Shore. With each new community, churches and schools were established, continuing the nationalistic culture and traditions of this active ethnic group.

Greek cuisine radically departs from others of Europe and closely resembles the foods of the Near East. These recipes are common to most Chicago/Greek tables and have often found their way into the cooking vernacular of non-Greek Chicago cooks as well.

Assumption Church, 601 S. Central

TARAMASALATA
(Caviar Dip)

Yield: 14 servings

7 slices stale white bread, trimmed
   of crusts
10 ounces salmon roe (red caviar)

1½ tablespoons onion, grated
⅓ cup olive oil
2 lemons, juiced

Soak the bread in a little water for 15 minutes; squeeze dry. Mix with the other ingredients and puree it to a smooth paste consistency. Chill.

AVGOLEMONO SOUPA
(Lemon and Egg Soup)

Yield: 6 to 8 servings

1 large stewing hen, cut up
1 carrot, chopped
1 stalk celery, chopped
1 onion, chopped
4 whole cloves
dash of salt
2 quarts water
½ cup rice
3 egg yolks
4 tablespoons freshly squeezed
   lemon juice

Place the chicken, carrot, celery, onion, cloves and salt in the water and simmer, covered, for about 1¼ hours until the chicken is very tender. Strain the broth, reserving the chicken for another use. Pour the broth into a kettle and boil down to about 1½ quarts. Add the rice and boil for 18 minutes. Beat the egg yolks and add a little broth to them, then add to the broth-rice mixture. Stir constantly over low heat until thickened. Turn off the heat and add the lemon juice. Serve.

SALATA HELLENIKI
(Greek Salad)

Yield: 6 servings

2 heads boston lettuce, chopped
1 head bib lettuce, chopped
3 tomatoes, quartered
1 large onion, sliced thinly
1 green pepper, diced
1 large cucumber, sliced thinly
6 anchovy fillets, minced
¾ cup olive oil
⅓ cup wine vinegar
pinch of sugar
salt and pepper
¼ teaspoon oregano
¼ teaspoon thyme
12 1-inch cubes feta cheese
12 black Greek olives

   Toss the vegetables and anchovies. Mix oil, vinegar, sugar, salt, pepper, spices. Toss with salad. Garnish with feta cheese and black olives. Serve cold.

PILAFI
(Rice)

Yield: 6 servings

1 cup uncooked rice
3 tablespoons butter, divided

2 cups chicken broth, or 2 chicken bouillon cubes in 2 cups water
1 teaspoon tomato paste

   Rinse the rice in a colander until the water runs clear. In saucepan, mix 1 tablespoon butter, broth and tomato paste and bring to a boil. Add the rice. Stir. Cover and cook on very low heat for 15 to 20 minutes until all water is absorbed. Do not remove the cover during cooking. Stir in 2 tablespoons butter and fluff. Let stand in warming oven, covered, for an additional 5 minutes.

PASTITSIO
(Baked Macaroni & Meat Sauce)

Yield: 6 to 8 servings

½ pound elbow macaroni
1 pound ground beef
1 large onion, chopped
¼ pound (1 stick) butter
1½ teaspoons cinnamon

salt and pepper
¾ cup water
2 cups hot milk
3 eggs, beaten
¾ cup grated cheese

Preheat oven to 325 degrees F.

Cook macaroni in boiling, salted water, according to package directions. Drain. Sauté meat and onion in butter until browned. Sprinkle with cinnamon and salt and pepper. Add tomato paste mixed with the water and simmer slowly until thick. In a small pan slowly add hot milk to the beaten eggs. Put half the macaroni into a greased pan (about 7-by-11 inches). Spread half the meat mixture over macaroni and sprinkle half the cheese on top; repeat procedure with the remaining half of recipe. Pour the egg mixture over top. Sprinkle on the remaining cheese. Bake for 30 minutes. Cut in squares and serve.

ARNI SOUVLAKIA
(Lamb Shish-kebobs)

Yield: 8 to 10 servings

1 4-pound leg of lamb cut in 2-inch
    cubes
salt, pepper, oregano

6 tablespoons olive oil
3 lemons, juiced

Marinate the lamb in a mixture of the spices, oil and lemon juice for 1 hour at room temperature, turning it often. Skewer the meat and broil close to the heat until outside is brown and inside pink, 10 to 12 minutes. Serve immediately over Pilafi.

The "give the lady what she wants" city

MOUSSAKA
(Eggplant-Lamb Casserole)

Yield: 8 to 10 servings

2 large eggplants
½ cup olive oil
½ cup butter
5 onions, chopped
2 cloves garlic, mashed
1½ pounds ground lamb
salt and pepper
½ teaspoon thyme
¾ cup wine
3 tomatoes, chopped and peeled
2 egg whites
¾ cup bread crumbs

Preheat oven to 350 degrees F.

Slice eggplants. Place in a colander, sprinkle with salt, and drain. Fry the eggplant slices, several at a time, in half of the oil and butter. Drain. Sauté onions and garlic in remaining oil and butter mixture until soft. Add meat, salt and pepper, thyme, wine and tomatoes. Simmer about 35 minutes. Let cool 5 minutes and add egg whites, stirring the mixture to blend. Add 1/3 of the crumbs. Stir, blending well. Place the rest of crumbs in a 2-quart casserole dish. Layer the eggplant and meat mixture into the dish, ending with eggplant. Pour 1½ cups **Béchamel Sauce** over eggplant and bake for 1 hour.

Béchamel Sauce

2 tablespoons butter
2 tablespoons flour
salt

1½ cups milk
2 egg yolks, beaten

Over medium heat make a roux of the butter and flour. Add salt and milk, stirring until thick. Add some warm sauce to the yolks, and then add the yolk mixture to the sauce.

KOTAPETA
(Chicken and Brains in Phyllo Pastry)

Yield: 10 servings

1 whole calf's brains
juice of one lemon
3 cups salted water
5 tablespoons vinegar
4 cups cooked chicken meat, diced
1 cup diced cooked ham

½ cup white wine
1 tablespoon butter
salt and pepper
16 leaves phyllo or strudel pastry
¾ cup melted butter

Preheat oven to 375 degrees F.

Soak the brains for 30 minutes in cold water to which lemon juice has been added. Drain brains, then boil in water and vinegar for 25 minutes. Remove from water, cool, and dice into small pieces. Combine the chicken, ham and brains. Cook in a skillet with the wine, butter, salt and pepper until the wine is reduced by at least one half. Place one sheet of pastry in a 10-by-13 inch baking pan and paint it with melted butter. Place another on top of the first and paint it with butter. Continue with eight sheets. Spread the meat mixture over the eighth sheet. Place the remaining eight sheets, buttering each, over the chicken mixture. Bake for 60 minutes until top is golden. Cool for 5 to 8 minutes and cut into diamond shapes. Serve.

—*Valerie Downes*

ARNI PSITO
(Lamb and Vegetable Roast)

Yield: 6 servings

1 6-pound leg of lamb
3 garlic cloves, cut up
olive oil
thyme
salt and pepper

1½ cups water
1½ tablespoons tomato paste
1 tablespoon lemon juice
6 medium potatoes, quartered
2 onions, quartered

Preheat oven to 325 degrees F.

Trim the lamb. Make pockets in the meat and insert the garlic pieces. Rub with oil and sprinkle with thyme, salt and pepper. Place in roasting pan in oven for 45 minutes. Mix water, tomato paste and lemon juice and baste roast with it. Roast for 1 hour. Add potatoes and onions. Cook for another 45 minutes uncovered.

BAKLAVA
(Almond and Walnut Pastry)

Yield: 10 to 12 servings

14 sheets of phyllo or strudel
   pastry
¾ cup melted butter
1 cup almonds, blanched and
   chopped
1 cup walnuts, blanched and
   chopped
1 cup honey
1½ cups sugar
1½ cups water
2 sticks cinnamon
3 lemon rinds
12 whole cloves

Preheat oven to 350 degrees F.

In a 10-by-10 inch greased baking pan layer ten sheets of pastry. Mix the nuts together. Paint sheets with melted butter and sprinkle with nuts. Bake for 50 minutes until golden. Cool. Combine the honey, nuts. Bake for 50 minutes until golden. Cool. Combine the honey, sugar, water, cinnamon and lemon rind. Boil 4 minutes. Remove the cinnamon and rind and continue to boil to the heavy syrup stage. Pour over phyllo and nuts. Cool for 15 minutes. Cut in diamond shapes. Place a whole clove in center of each diamond. Serve at room temperature.

—George Drew

The Hungarians

In the middle of the nineteenth century, political upheavals in their native land forced many Hungarians to seek refuge elsewhere. Some found their way to Chicago in the 1850s, and by 1870 this little community of immigrants numbered almost 200.

Some of these new Chicagoans made immediate contributions to the developing city in business, trade and education. Chicago's first private foreign language school was established by a member of this community as early as the mid-1850s. Soon, the military experience of several of the new Hungarian-Chicagoans became of great use to the Chicago military units which fought in the Civil War, contributing to their success and valor.

As Chicago approached the turn of the century, the Hungarian community numbered almost 7,500 in its foreign born and first generation population. Most of its members were Catholic, but some worshipped in the Jewish faith and in other denominations. The first Roman Catholic Church built for Chicago's Hungarian population was constructed in 1904 and was located at 91st Street and Avalon Road. Cultural contributions were being made in theatrical and journalistic circles as the flair of this nationality group put its stamp on Chicago's development.

European wars and political unrest resulted in a significant upsurge in the number of Hungarians in the first two decades of the twentieth century. By 1920, the Hungarian foreign-born and first generation American population had soared to almost 30,500. And although new population centers had sprung up on the near north side and in other parts of the city, the principal center of this group remained most concentrated in the area of the south east side where its first nationalistic church had been built.

Although Hungarian food shares much with its Slavic and Austrian neighbors, it has many dishes which have a distinctiveness of their own. For example, the deft employment of fresh paprika in many tempting dishes is uniquely Hungarian.

St. Stephen of Hungary Church at 2015 W. Augusta

KÖROZÖTT LIPTOI
(Anchovy Cheese Spread)

Yield: 2½ cups

1 cup pot cheese
3 anchovy fillets, wiped of oil
½ pound (2 sticks) butter
1½ tablespoons caraway seeds
1 tablespoon capers, minced

1½ tablespoons scallion tops, minced
¾ tablespoon dry mustard
parsley and fresh paprika

Sieve the cheese. Mash the anchovies. Cream the butter with caraway, capers, scallions and mustard. Add the anchovies and cheese; mix until smooth. Garnish with parsley and paprika. Ricotta cheese, farmer's cheese, or cottage cheese—well-drained—may be substituted for pot cheese.

KÖMÉNYMAGOS LEVES
(Caraway Broth)

Yield: 6 to 8 servings

¼ cup chicken fat, though fat of any fowl may be used
½ cup flour
6 cups water

salt (to taste)
4 tablespoons caraway seeds
parsley, chopped

In a large pot make a roux of the fat and flour. Stir constantly until golden brown. Stir in the water and the salt. Add the caraway. Bring to the boil and simmer for 15 minutes. Strain. Decorate with the parsley and serve.

American Indians often smoked their meats to preserve them. Fish from Lake Michigan, waterfowl and game were cut in chunks and impaled on stakes before a green wood fire.

MÉZESKÁLACS
(Honey Bread)

Yield: 1 loaf

½ pound honey
¾ cup sugar, divided
4 eggs, separated
¾ teaspoon cloves
¾ teaspoon cinnamon
½ lemon rind, grated
1 tablespoon vanilla extract
½ pound rye flour
1 teaspoon baking powder
1½ tablespoons butter
almonds, blanched
milk

Preheat oven to 350 degrees F.

Heat honey in saucepan to lukewarm. Add ½ cup sugar and egg yolks. Beat. Remove from heat and add spices, lemon, and vanilla; beat again. Stir flour and baking powder together and beat into honey mixture. Beat the egg whites until stiff and gently fold in. Pour the batter into a 9-by-13-inch loaf pan buttered with 1½ tablespoons of butter and spread evenly. Decorate with almonds and bake 30 minutes. Take from oven and brush with the milk and remaining sugar. Cut and serve.

PAPRIKASALATA
(Pepper Salad)

Yield: 6 servings

6 whole green peppers
½ cup dry white wine
4 tablespoons lemon juice
4 tablespoons water

1 teaspoon sugar
salt and pepper
1 cup freshly made mayonnaise or
   sour cream

Preheat the oven to 450 degrees F.

Roast the peppers on a rack in the oven until skin blisters and begins to turn black. Remove from oven, peel, and discard seeds. Cut peppers in long strips. Mix the rest of the ingredients except the mayonnaise and pour over the peppers. Let them marinate in the refrigerator overnight. Drain them. Toss with mayonnaise and serve.

PARADICSOMOS KÁPOSZTA
(Tomato Cabbage)

Yield: 6 servings

1 large head cabbage, chopped
water
3 tablespoons butter
1½ tablespoons flour
4 cups tomato juice
½ teaspoon fresh paprika
1 large onion, diced
1 green pepper, diced
salt and pepper
1 teaspoon sugar

Cover cabbage with water and cook until tender. Drain. In a skillet, make a roux of butter and flour. Add the tomato juice and paprika; stir until slightly thickened. Put the cabbage in a pot and add the thickened tomato juice, onion, green pepper, salt, pepper and sugar. Stir. Simmer uncovered, stirring occasionally until thickened, about 12 to 15 minutes.

The "I will" city

BURGONYAKÉREG
(Molded Potatoes)

Yield: 6 to 8 servings

1 pound of potatoes
3 small eggs
2½ tablespoons butter
salt and pepper

Boil the potatoes; peel and rice them. Preheat oven to 375 degrees F. Add the other ingredients to the potatoes and whip the mixture. Butter muffin tins and dollop in the potatoes, pressing down to completely fill the mold. Bake for 15 minutes. Remove potatoes from muffin molds and serve.

CSIPETKE
(Pinch Dumplings)

Yield: 8 servings

6 eggs
4 cups flour, sifted
½ teaspoon salt
6 slices bacon

1 cup sour cream
¼ pound pot cheese
¼ teaspoon white pepper

Mix the eggs, flour and salt together. Knead to a stiff dough, about 2 minutes. Divide the dough and make finger-thick strands. Pinch off the dough in small pieces and place into 4 quarts of rapidly boiling salted water. When they rise to the surface, they are done. Fry the bacon until crisp. Remove from skillet and crumble. Fry the boiled dumplings in the bacon fat. When they are browned, remove to a bowl.

Crumble the cheese and mix with the dumplings. Mix in the sour cream. Place on a serving dish, sprinkle with pepper, and spread the bacon over the top.

SZÉKELY GULYAS
(Goulash)

Yield: 6 to 8 servings

2 pounds pork, cut in 2-inch cubes
3 tablespoons vinegar
1 pound sauerkraut
2½ cups water
1 green pepper, seeded and sliced

1½ teaspoons caraway seeds
1½ tablespoons tomato paste or puree
salt
½ cup sour cream

Rub the pork cubes with the vinegar and let stand for 1 hour. Wash and drain the sauerkraut. Place everything except the sour cream, meat last, into a slow cooker. Cook on low (200 degrees F.) for 8 hours. Swirl in the sour cream. Serve. If the Goulash is made in a Dutch oven, brown the pork cubes first, and add the sauerkraut 45 minutes after the other ingredients and cook until tender.

—Sue Rusnak

The Hungarian festival, the Celebration of the Harvesting of the Grapes, is held in early October. The festival is sponsored by the Calvin Hungarian United Church of Christ. Folk dancing is a major feature of the festival and a Csardas is the opening dance. It is led by the oldest married couple at the celebration. Delectable Hungarian food is the highlight of the festivities and include such gastronomic delights as houka, a kind of sausage; palacsintas; and world-renowned Dobos tortes.

FÁCÁN
(Roast Pheasant)

Yield: 2 servings

1 2-pound pheasant, prepared for
  cooking
salt

1 pound bacon, sliced
⅓ cup sour cream
1 large onion, sliced

    Preheat oven to 450 degrees F.
    Salt the pheasant inside. Using toothpicks to hold the bacon together, wrap the pheasant in the slices. Place in a roasting pan, cover and roast 15 minutes. Turn the oven down to 375 degrees F. Take roaster from oven and spread sour cream over the pheasant. Arrange onion slices on top of sour cream. Cover and roast for 40 minutes at 375 degrees F.

CITROMOS MARHAHÚS
(Lemony Beef)

Yield: 4 servings

2 pounds lean beef, cubed
1 cup broth
6 slices bacon
1 tablespoon bacon fat
1 tablespoon flour
2 tablespoons lemon juice
⅓ teaspoon sugar
1 tablespoon sweet basil
1½ cups sour cream

    Simmer the beef in the broth in a covered pot until tender, about 1 hour. Fry the bacon until crisp. Remove it from the pan, crumble it and set aside. Remove the beef from the broth and let cool. Make a roux of 1 tablespoon bacon fat (reserving the rest of the fat) and flour in a skillet. Stir the cooled broth into the roux, then add the lemon juice, sugar and basil. Add the beef to the bacon drippings left in the pan and heat thoroughly. Swirl the sour cream into the thickened mixture and pour over beef. Place on a serving plate and sprinkle the crumbled bacon over it.

ALMÁS SUTÉMENYE
(Apple Cookies)

Yield: 12 pieces

2 cups flour
2 teaspoons baking powder
1 cup butter
1 cup sugar plus ¼ cup for apples
3 egg yolks

1 lemon rind, grated
1 cup dry bread crumbs
1 teaspoon cinnamon
2 or 3 large apples, shredded
1 cup ground nut meats

Preheat oven to 350 degrees F.

Sift together flour and baking powder. In separate bowl, cream butter and 1 cup sugar together; add egg yolks, rind and flour mixture. Add bread crumbs and cinnamon. Spread in greased 12-by-7-by-2-inch pan, reserving half for the topping. Cover with sliced apples, and sprinkle on some cinnamon and sugar to sweeten apples. Place the nuts and reserved crumbs on top and bake for 1 hour, until lightly browned all over. Cool in pan at least 10 minutes before cutting in squares.

In 1837 there were nineteen grocery and provision stores and ten taverns thriving in Chicago.

Diamond Jim Brady and Lillian Russell were as much an attraction at the World Columbian Exposition in 1893 as the newly invented Ferris Wheel. They were gawked at by tourists when they dined out on their favorite food: sweet corn, dripping with butter.

"There's nothing wrong with nepotism as long as you keep it in the family"

—*Richard J. Daley*

Of course, St. Patrick's Day represents the principal day of celebration for the Irish. Until a few years ago, there were several parades celebrating this Irish holiday in the various Irish ethnic centers of Chicago. But under the regime of the late Mayor Daly, these were consolidated into the grand and glorious celebration which features a march down State Street every March 17th. For the occasion, the center stripe of that noble thoroughfare is painted green, and the Chicago River is dyed green. A queen is selected from the Chicago Irish population to preside over the festivities, where traditional Irish food and green beer are served.

The Irish

The original Irish population in Chicago numbered about 900 in 1836 when construction work began on the Illinois-Michigan Canal. Many of them were hired by agents sent from Chicago to Europe exclusively for this purpose. Whole families traveled by ship for weeks to the eastern shores of the United States and then continued their journey by rail and on the newly developed steamships through the Great Lakes to land at the harbor of Chicago. Like the Germans, the Irish settled along the South Fork of the Chicago River near the construction of the canal. The area was a part of the Bridgeport farm referred to as "Hardscrabble."

St. Patrick's Church, one of the first of Chicago's many nationalistic parish churches, was erected in 1846 on DesPlaines Street, between Washington and Randolph. The church demonstrates unmistakably the culture of its early parishioners in the depiction of Irish saints and the Celtic theme of its decoration.

Their spiritual needs tended to, several enterprising members of the Irish community established and profited by saloons and pubs which provided relaxation and enjoyment after the exhausting labors at the canal construction site.

Although many of the Irish and their progeny remained in the location of the original settlement, others began to move out and farther away from the congestion of the central city. The potato famine of 1848, and other political, religious and economic reversals in Ireland increased and intensified the flow of Irish immigration. Newcomers began to form new communities on the far south, the west, and in scattered areas of the north side of the city, and the constituents soon became actively involved in the economic, political, cultural and religious development of Chicago. By 1870, the Irish numbered 39,000, and in 1890 there were over 246,000 foreign-born Irish and their children in Chicago.

Irish food is a hearty peasant cuisine, and as such depends largely on the food at hand for its character. Breakfast and tea breads, boiled meats, dairy products and plain desserts make up the basis of Irish meals. The lowly potato can be found on almost every table, and the Irish certainly have a way with it.

Celtic cross on the exterior of St. Patrick's Church at 718 W. Adams

BARM BRACK

Yield: 2 round loaves

4 cups sifted flour
½ teaspoon salt
½ teaspoon cinnamon
⅛ teaspoon mace
¼ teaspoon nutmeg
4 tablespoons (½ stick) butter
¾ cup sugar
1 cake yeast
1 cup lukewarm milk
1 egg, beaten
1 cup white raisins
1½ cups currants
⅔ cup citron or candied lemon or
    orange peel

Be sure that all utensils are at room temperature before the preparation is begun. Sift together flour, salt and spices. Blend in butter with fork until mixture is full of fine lumps. Add all but 1 teaspoon of sugar and blend well. In large bowl, blend yeast with 1 teaspoon sugar and 1 teaspoon lukewarm milk. Mix remaining lukewarm milk and egg together. Add to yeast mixture. Gradually beat flour mixture into yeast mixture. With a long-handled wooden spoon, mix until dough is stiff but elastic. Add fruit and mix thoroughly. Cover dough with a fresh linen tea towel and place in warm place until doubled in size, about 1 hour. Punch dough down and turn onto lightly floured surface. Coat 2 cake tins with butter. Divide dough and place in 8- or 9-inch round cake tins and let rise for 30 minutes. Preheat oven to 400 degrees F. Bake for 1 hour or until golden and crusty on top.

—*Wynne Callaghan*

The train carrying Gould, Pullman and Vanderbilt, and the Golden Spike with which they would join the rail lines from coast to coast, was equipped by Chicago restaurateur Kinsley with the most elegant dinner service and supplied with food fit for kings, as, of course, they were.

IRISH SCONES

Yield: 2 dozen

3 cups sifted flour
2½ teaspoons baking powder
½ cup sugar
½ teaspoon baking soda
1 teaspoon salt
¾ cup butter
¾ cup currants
1 cup buttermilk
¼ cup light cream
¼ cup sugar

Preheat oven to 450 degrees F.
Combine dry ingredients in a bowl, cutting in butter until mixture is well blended. Add currants gradually, then buttermilk. When dough is thoroughly mixed, place on floured board. Shape into oblong biscuits about 2 inches long and 1½ inches wide. Place on buttered baking sheet. Brush tops with cream and sprinkle with sugar. Bake for 15 minutes. Serve warm.

—*Kate Jennings*

PUREED KALE

Yield: 4 servings

1 pound kale leaves, washed and
   stripped from stalk
½ teaspoon salt

pinch of pepper
3 tablespoons butter
4 tablespoons heavy cream

Boil kale leaves in lightly salted water to cover until tender. Preheat oven to 350 degrees F. Puree cooked kale in blender or food mill. Add salt and pepper, butter, and cream. Put into a 1-to-1½-quart casserole dish. Heat for 25 to 30 minutes.

TOMATOES AND SPRING ONIONS

Yield: 4 servings

3 large tomatoes, cut into thick
   slices
½ cup green onions, chopped fine
½ teaspoon salt
¼ teaspoon pepper
¼ cup salad oil
juice of 1 lemon
fresh mint leaves

Overlap tomato slices on platter. Sprinkle chopped onion over. Add salt and pepper. Drizzle oil over tomatoes, then sprinkle lemon juice on top. Scatter with mint leaves.

COLCANNON

Yield: 4 to 6 servings

1 pound cabbage, chopped
4 medium potatoes, peeled and
   diced
2 green onions, chopped

1 cup heavy cream
¼ pound (1 stick) butter
salt and pepper
mace

Boil cabbage and potatoes in separate pots in lightly salted water to cover, until tender. Drain. Simmer onions in cream. Mash potatoes and mix together with butter and onion-cream mixture; salt and pepper to taste. Add drained cabbage and mace to taste. Keep warm over low heat until ready to serve.

—Alice O'Donnell

MASHED RUTABAGA

Yield: 6 to 8 servings

2 large rutabagas, peeled and diced
juice of 1 lemon
½ cup butter
¾ cup heavy cream

1 teaspoon salt
½ teaspoon white pepper
¼ teaspoon nutmeg

Place rutabagas in saucepan. Cover with lightly salted water. Add lemon juice, and boil until tender. Drain. Mash rutabagas with butter, fold in cream, and salt, pepper and nutmeg.

—Mary Lou Leonard

ROLLED SOLE FILLETS IN CUSTARD

Yield: 6 servings

6 fillets of sole
lemon juice
salt and pepper
½ cup chopped onion
2 eggs
1½ cups milk
butter

Soak sole fillets in water until freshened. Drain and dry. Preheat oven to 325 degrees F. Roll fillets and fasten with toothpicks. Place in buttered, heavy 2-inch deep baking pan. Sprinkle with lemon juice, salt and pepper. Scatter chopped onion over. Beat eggs and milk together; pour over rolled fillets. Dot with butter. Bake for 45 minutes until set. Allow to cool for 10 minutes before serving. Garnish with lemon slices.

—Anne Barrett

SMOKED BUTT WITH CABBAGE

Yield: 6 servings

1 2½- to 3-pound smoked butt
¼ cup brown sugar
1 tablespoon dry mustard

1 clove garlic
1 large head cabbage, quartered
¼ cup (½ stick) butter

Place meat in large kettle. Cover with water and add sugar, mustard and garlic. Bring to a boil and simmer for 1 hour. Remove meat from liquid and keep warm. Place cabbage in liquid and cook over moderate heat for about 15 minutes until cabbage is tender. Drain cabbage; mix with butter. Arrange on platter around slices of meat.

—*Marian Callaghan*

LAMB STEW

Yield: 6 servings

4 tablespoons flour
1 teaspoon salt
¼ teaspoon pepper
4 tablespoons cooking oil
3 pounds lamb stew meat, cut into
   2-inch pieces
1 medium onion, chopped
2 carrots, scraped and sliced

3 turnips, cubed
1 stalk celery, chopped
1½ cups shredded cabbage
4 potatoes, peeled and cubed
10 peppercorns
1 bay leaf
1 tablespoon dried parsley flakes

Mix flour, salt and pepper together. Heat oil in large saucepan. Coat lamb pieces with flour mixture and brown on all sides in hot oil. Add onions and cook for a few minutes until onions are soft. Add all remaining ingredients and add water to barely cover. Bring to a boil, cover, and simmer for 2 hours. Check seasoning. Remove bay leaf, sprinkle with parsley and serve.

—*Winnefred Whalen*

BLACKBERRY COBBLER

Yield: 6 servings

1¼ cups flour
1 tablespoon sugar
1½ teaspoons baking powder
¼ teaspoon salt
⅛ teaspoon mace
3 tablespoons softened butter, divided

½ cup milk
2 cups blackberries
¾ cup sugar
juice of ½ lemon
pinch of salt
1 tablespoon flour
1 cup heavy cream

Preheat oven to 400 degrees F.

Sift first five ingredients together. Cut in 2 tablespoons of the butter. Add milk gradually, blending until soft dough is formed. Mix berries, sugar, lemon juice, salt and flour. Pour into buttered 1½ quart baking dish. Spread cobbler dough over top. Brush with remaining tablespoon of butter. Bake for 40 minutes or until crust is delicately browned. Serve with heavy cream.

—*Mary Quinn*

LEMON JUMP-UP

Yield: 6 servings

3 tablespoons flour
1 cup sugar
1 cup milk
2 eggs, separated
juice and grated rind of 1 lemon
whipped cream

Preheat oven to 375 degrees F.

Mix together flour, sugar, milk, egg yolks, lemon juice and rind. Beat egg whites until stiff and fold in. Turn mixture into buttered 1½ quart baking dish. Place dish in pan of hot water. Bake for 1 hour or until cake has left sides of pan. Spoon out to serve, either warm or cool, topped with whipped cream.

—*Celine Hoskins*

The Italians

The first Italians in Chicago numbered about one hundred when they took up residence along the south bank of the Chicago River in the area referred to as South Water Market. It was an insignificant number in comparison to the large numbers of this nationality who would call Chicago their home some fifty years hence.

Because of the unusual political structure they had left behind, these new arrivals often clung to regional Italian ties instead of nationalistic ones. The new churches and schools which they built often reflected this in the inclusion of the names of the provinces from which they came. Churches with the names of Our Lady of Pompeii and St. Phillip Benizi exemplified the provincial patriotism of their parishioners.

As these new Americans came to Chicago, they began to establish population centers on the near north side, in the Loop and the near west side. Mutual benefit societies were organized to help the less fortunate, the elderly, the sick and the orphaned. Mother Frances Cabrini, one of the most active participants in caring for these charitable concerns, became the first American saint of the Roman Catholic Church.

The arts in Chicago were considerably enriched by this immigrant group, too. An Italo-Chicagoan, Cleofonte Campanini, was responsible for the development of one of Chicago's first opera companies. Sculptors and architects, reflecting the rich cultural traditions of their artistic heritage, added to the aesthetic growth of the city, and the first Italian newspaper, *l'Italia,* outdid even its New York counterpart in circulation.

By 1920, Chicagoans of Italian birth and their children made up a community of about 124,000 people, their numbers scattered from north to south both inside and outside the city limits.

Many Italian dishes have crossed over into the American food repertoire so completely that they are no longer considered Italian. Like the development of the early population centers, many of these dishes retain a provincial flavor while maintaining a basic and unmistakable Italian character.

Italian sausage and specialty shop in Elmwood Park

BAGNO CALDO
(Anchovy Dip)

Yield: 8 to 10 servings

2 cups butter
6 garlic cloves, mashed
2 cans anchovies in olive oil
2 green peppers, cut in strips

1 bunch celery, cleaned
20 cauliflower flowerettes
1 loaf Italian bread, cut into 20 chunks

Melt the butter in a fondue pan. Add the garlic and anchovies. Stir until the anchovies disintegrate, being careful not to let the butter brown. Arrange the vegetables and bread on a plate surrounding the fondue pan.

CROSTINI
(Paté Appetizer)

Yield: 28 to 36 pieces

¼ cup butter, softened
½ loaf French bread, sliced into ½-inch thick pieces

1 tin liver paté
2 tablespoons olive oil
3 tablespoons chopped fresh basil

Preheat oven to broil.
Spread softened butter on each bread round; spread thinly with liver pate. Sprinkle each with a few drops of olive oil and a pinch of chopped basil. Place under broiler for 8 to 10 minutes. Serve hot.

The extremely heavy cream that early Chicagoans used resulted from letting the separated cream rest, covered, in a cool place. To make a reasonable facsimile of that cream, mix one tablespoon buttermilk with one cup cream and heat the mixture to lukewarm. Pour into a glass container, cover with waxed paper and place in a cool (60 to 75 degrees F.) location. Cream will thicken in 10 to 20 hours. When thick, refrigerate. It will last 7 to 10 days.

MINESTRONE
(Vegetable Soup)

Yield: 10 to 12 servings

1 pound shin beef with bone
3½ quarts water
2 tablespoons salt
½ teaspoon pepper
1 cup kidney beans
2 cloves garlic
1 tablespoon olive oil
½ cup onion, chopped
½ cup parsley, chopped

1 cup fresh green beans, cut up
¾ cup celery, diced
1 cup peas
2 cups cabbage, chopped
1 cup carrots, diced
1 can tomato sauce
½ cup spaghetti, broken into small
   pieces
Parmesan cheese, grated

Combine beef with water, salt, pepper and beans; cover and bring to a boil. Skim off fat, cover, and simmer 3 hours. Brown garlic in hot oil. Remove garlic and sauté onions and parsley until onions are tender. Remove meat from stock and reserve for use in another dish; add onions, parsley, and remaining ingredients, except spaghetti and cheese. Cover and simmer 30 minutes. Add spaghetti and cook 10 minutes. Serve sprinkled with cheese.

—Sharon Anzalone

FAGIOLINI AL SUGO
(Green Beans in Tomato Sauce)

Yield: 4 servings

2 cloves garlic, sliced
4 tablespoons Lucca olive oil
1 pound washed and trimmed
   fresh green beans

½ teaspoon salt
¼ teaspoon pepper
½ teaspoon dried sage
1 small can tomato sauce

Sauté sliced garlic in olive oil until slightly brown. Remove garlic pieces and add beans, salt, pepper and sage. Mix well. Blend in tomato sauce, cover, and cook over low heat for about 20 minutes until beans are tender.

—James Hogan

UOVA IN SALSA VERDE
(Eggs in Green Sauce)

Yield: 6 servings

1 good-size bunch of watercress
4 sprigs parsley
6 tablespoons very heavy cream
2 cups homemade mayonnaise
1 teaspoon chervil
12 hard-boiled eggs, peeled

Chop watercress and parsley fine, or put in food processor. Fold cream into mayonnaise. Add chervil, parsley and watercress, blending thoroughly. Slice a small piece from the side of each egg and place sliced side down on a serving dish. Pour sauce over eggs, coating each completely. Garnish with leftover watercress leaves.

ZUCCHINI ALLA PARMIGIANA
(Zucchini with Cheese and Tomato)

Yield: 4 to 6 servings

¼ cup olive oil
2 cloves garlic, minced
3 medium zucchini, scrubbed, washed and sliced ½-inch thick
2 6-ounce cans tomato sauce

¾ cup freshly grated Parmesan cheese
½ cup freshly chopped basil
1 tablespoon butter

Preheat oven to 375 degrees F.

Heat oil in a large skillet and sauté garlic until light brown. Add zucchini slices and cook on both sides until golden. Remove zucchini with slotted spoon to a flat surface, draining as much oil as possible. Use 1 tablespoon butter to grease a wide 1½-quart casserole. Place a layer of zucchini on the bottom, then spoon over tomato sauce to cover. Sprinkle with 1/3 of the grated Parmesan cheese and top with 1/3 of the chopped basil. Make two more layers in the same manner and bake for 25 minutes.

CARCIOFI RIPIENI
(Stuffed Artichokes)

Yield: 6 servings

To prepare 6 artichokes for stuffing, cut 1 inch off each top. Cut off stems and remove outside lower leaves and thorny leaf tips. Turn artichokes stem side up on firm surface and hammer with hand. This will open artichoke. Remove and discard fuzzy choke. Soak artichoke in cold water. Drain and stuff.

Stuffing

2 cups fresh bread crumbs	pinch each of salt and pepper
1 whole egg	1 teaspoon oregano
⅓ cup grated Romano cheese	⅓ cup olive oil
1 tablespoon parsley	1 1-pound can whole tomatoes
1 clove garlic, minced	

Mash ½ of the tomatoes. Mix all ingredients together, reserving unmashed tomatoes. Pack into center of each artichoke. Fill to top. Stand artichokes in heavy pot, stem down. Top with remaining ½ can tomatoes, mashed, and 2 or 3 tablespoons oil and ¼ cup water. Cover and simmer for 2 hours or until tender.

—Christine Correlli

By 1926, there were twenty thousand speakeasies in Chicago to wet the palates of the anti-prohibitionists. In that year, illegal booze brought sixty million dollars into syndicate coffers.

PASTA E FAGIOLI
(Pasta with Beans)

Yield: 6 to 8 servings

1 pound macaroni
1 20-ounce can baby lima beans or
   butter beans
2 garlic cloves
1 cup Lucca olive oil
2 tablespoons salt
pepper

Cook macaroni in boiling, salted water, according to package directions. Drain. Add lima beans. Fry garlic cloves in hot oil until garlic is dark brown. Remove garlic and discard. Add hot oil to macaroni mixture. Sprinkle black pepper on top and serve immediately.

LASAGNE VERDE BOLOGNESE
(Green Lasagne)

Meat Sauce

Yield: 6 servings

½ cup Lucca olive oil
2 onions, minced
1 carrot, minced
1 stalk celery, minced
1½ teaspoons parsley
1 clove
½ pound chopped uncooked
   chicken livers

¾ pound finely ground beef
¾ pound finely ground pork
1 cup dry red wine
2 cups beef broth
1 tablespoon tomato paste
1 teaspoon salt
½ teaspoon pepper
½ cup cream

Heat oil in saucepan and add onions, carrot, celery, parsley, and clove. Sauté vegetables until softened but not brown. Add chicken livers, mixing thoroughly. Add beef and pork and brown lightly. Add wine and turn heat up to cook the mixture briskly and evaporate the wine. Add broth. Stir in tomato paste, salt and pepper. Let simmer over low heat for about 2 hours. If liquid evaporates too quickly, add a little water. Remove from heat and swirl in cream.

1 cup freshly grated Romano cheese
2 pounds cooked green noodles (the wider and flatter, the better)
3 cups **Béchamel Sauce** (recipe page 82), to which 1½ teaspoons nutmeg have been added
2 tablespoons butter

Preheat oven to 400 degrees F.

Reserve 2 tablespoons of grated cheese. Place a layer of noodles in a buttered 13-by-7-inch baking dish, cover with 1/3 of the meat sauce, sprinkle with 1/3 of the grated cheese and top with 1/3 of the béchamel sauce. Make 2 more layers. Dot the top layer with bits of the 2 tablespoons of butter and sprinkle with the 2 remaining tablespoons of cheese. Cover with foil and bake for 20 minutes. Remove foil and bake for 20 minutes. Remove foil and bake for another 10 minutes until sauce is bubbling but not browned.

CALZONE
(Stuffed Pizza)

Yield: 12 servings

1 cake yeast
1 cup lukewarm water
4 cups flour
1 teaspoon salt
2 tablespoons olive oil

Dissolve yeast in water. In separate bowl, make well in center of flour and add salt and yeast mixture. Turn onto board and knead for 10 minutes. Add oil and knead until smooth. Place in bowl, cover with a towel, and set in warm place to let rise for 2 hours. Punch down and roll out. Spread 2/3 of dough in well-greased baking pan, 11-by-15-by-3-inches deep, bringing sides of dough up to top edges of pan.

Filling

2½ pounds Italian sausage	½ cup grated Romano cheese
2 pounds ricotta cheese	½ cup minced parsley
6 eggs	salt and pepper

Preheat oven to 400 degrees F.

Cut sausage in ¼-inch pieces. Brown until done. Remove from pan and drain on towel. Cream ricotta in large bowl and add eggs one at a time, blending well after each addition. Add cheese, parsley, salt and pepper and mix well. Mix in sausage. Spread mixture evenly over dough. Roll remaining dough to fit over bottom crust. Prick dough all over with a fork and place over the filling in the pan. Go around edges with a fork to seal. Bake for 30 to 35 minutes or until golden brown. Remove from oven and cut into squares.

POLLO VESUVIO
(Chicken Vesuvio)

Yield: 4 servings

1 3-pound frying chicken, cut up	2 cloves garlic, mashed
¼ cup olive oil	2 teaspoons oregano
½ cup water	½ teaspoon sweet basil
½ cup red wine	

Brown chicken in oil. Lower heat and add water, wine and seasonings. Cover and simmer for 1 hour or until tender. Serve.

—William Massarelli

GRANITA DI CAFFE CON PANNA
(Coffee Ice with Heavy Cream)

Yield: 6 servings

1 cup sugar
2¼ cups water
2½ cups very strong black coffee
1½ cups heavy cream

Dissolve sugar in water. Boil until mixture is reduced by about one-third. Add the coffee and boil for another 3 minutes. Cool and pour mixture into a tray and freeze. When frozen, crush mixture and spoon into sherbet glasses. Top with heavy cream.

ZABAIONE
(Wine Custard)

Yield: 8 servings

¾ cup sugar
8 egg yolks
1¼ cups Marsala wine

Beat sugar and egg yolks together in top of double boiler until light and foamy, about 1 minute. Blend in Marsala wine. Place double boiler over medium low heat and beat with electric mixer until mixture thickens. When mixture begins to puff up, remove from heat. Serve warm in sherbet glasses.

MERINGHATA
(Whipped Cream Meringue Dessert)

Yield: 6 servings

3 cups whipping cream
2 teaspoons vanilla
½ cup powdered sugar
8 ounces shaved sweet chocolate
2 8-inch round meringue rounds

Whip cream until firm. Fold in vanilla and powdered sugar. Gently add shaved chocolate. Place 1 meringue round on cake dish and pile with ½ the whipped cream. Place second meringue round on top and cover with remaining whipped cream. Slice in wedges and serve.

Meringue

Yield: 2 8-inch meringue rounds

4 egg whites
1 cup sugar, divided
1 teaspoon vanilla

Preheat oven to 250 degrees F.

Beat egg whites until very stiff. Continue beating and add ¾ cup sugar, little by little. When egg whites are stiff and dry, add vanilla. Gently fold in the remaining ¼ cup sugar. Line a cookie sheet with brown paper. With a spoon, shape meringue mixture into 2 rounds, 8 inches in diameter. Bake for 1 hour until meringue is slightly colored and very dry.

"I saw a man; he danced with his wife"

Our Lady of Mt. Carmel is a fascinating Italian festival held in mid-July in Melrose Park. There is a parade which includes two Italian bands, church religious societies chanting prayers, and decorated statues carried on litters. A giant replica of Our Lady of Mt. Carmel is the dominant litter-borne statue and is the object of veneration. Flocks of the faithful follow behind the parade with lighted candles to its terminus at the church where an outdoor mass is held. Carnival rides, booths with delectable Italian food and souvenir vendors surround the church in which one may light candles for special causes.

The Japanese

There were two Japanese in Chicago when, in the 1880s, an American firm with both San Francisco and Chicago affiliates began a marketing campaign to familiarize Americans with Japanese arts and manufactured goods. In the true spirit of American enterprise, this firm sought to capture the potential market for Japanese wares soon to be released in foreign markets as a result of mutual trade agreements. The project held prophetic implications for the economic interdependence of the two countries a century later!

Growth of the Japanese community was slower than that of other immigrant groups, and by 1930 only 480 Japanese-Americans were divided among the three small settlements in Hyde Park, on the near north side and the near west side. Religious centers, both Buddhist and Christian, were established. Some of the newcomers went into service occupations, while others opened small businesses.

World War II effected a change on all Japanese settlements in the United States. New laws required the relocation of these Americans to the central sections of the country. Suddenly, in the 1940s, Chicago's Japanese population soared to 30,000, making it the largest mainland population center. And the city profited by the contributions of those for whom it provided refuge; bonsai, Japanese flower arrangements, and calligraphy became familiar additions to the Chicago vocabulary. New religious centers were established, as were schools and small businesses, each bringing the exotic cultural heritage of the islands in the Pacific to Chicago.

The large numbers of this immigrant group shifted somewhat and dissipated considerably after World War II. By 1970, the number of Japanese foreign-born and their children was 7,370, and most of these were settled in the Uptown area.

Japanese cuisine is delicate and haunting. Like the tea ceremony, it represents an appeal to the mind and to the eye as well as to the palate. It reflects the taste of its originators in the attention to detail represented in color combinations and its attractive arrangement on a plate.

Midwest Buddhist Temple at 435 W. Menomonee in Old Town

AWABI GOMU ZU
(Fish Salad)

Yield: 6 servings

1 cucumber, peeled
dash salt
1 can abalone

Dressing

3 tablespoons vinegar
2 tablespoons sugar

1 tablespoon water
1 tablespoon sesame seeds, toasted

Cut cucumber in half lengthwise. Remove seeds and slice thinly. Place in shallow dish; sprinkle with salt. Let sit for half an hour. Drain well. Wash lightly with cold water; drain again. Slice abalone thin. Gently mix with cucumber. Make dressing by combining vinegar, sugar and water. Lightly crush sesame seeds to release flavor; stir into vinegar mixture. Pour dressing over cucumber and abalone. Chill until ready to serve.

KIMUZU
(Salad Dressing)

Yield: 2 cups

1½ teaspoons dry mustard
1½ tablespoons corn flour
1½ tablespoons sugar

3 tablespoons vinegar
1 cup water
3 egg yolks

Sift dry mustard and corn flour together. Add salt and blend in vinegar. Gradually add water, stirring to prevent lumps. With electric beater, beat mixture. Add egg yolks, one at a time, beating thoroughly after each egg is added. Beat until smooth and creamy. Pour mixture into saucepan and cook over very low heat, stirring constantly until mixture is thickened but not simmering. Remove from heat and continue stirring until thick and smooth. Chill and serve over raw vegetable salad.

NAMASU
(Radish and Cabbage Salad)

Yield: 4 servings

2 cups raw, shredded cabbage
1½ cups radishes, thinly sliced

1 carrot, scraped and cut in julienne
   strips

Crisp all ingredients in ice water for 2 hours. Drain. Serve with Kimuzu Dressing.

GOHAN
(Rice)

Yield: 6 servings (about 1 cup each)

2½ cups medium grain rice
3 cups cold water

Wash rice, drain well. Put rice in heavy pan with close fitting lid. Add water, bring quickly to boiling. Cover pan, reduce heat and cook for 15 minutes. Turn heat to high for 10 to 15 seconds. Remove from heat. Do not stir or remove cover. Let sit for 10 minutes before serving.

Convention capital of the world

TEMPURA
(Deep Fried Sea Food and Vegetables)

Yield: 4 to 6 servings

10 to 14 medium shrimp
1 pound fillet of fish
1 (20-ounce) can tiny corn cobs
1 lotus root
3 bamboo shoots
1 can ginkgo nuts
6 green onions
½ pound fresh mushrooms
4 cups vegetable oil

Shell shrimp. Wash well and remove vein. Cut fish into bite-size pieces. Drain canned vegetables and dry thoroughly. Slice lotus root and bamboo shoots thinly. Put 2 to 3 nuts on strong wooden toothpicks. Cut onions in bite-size pieces. Halve mushrooms. Place all above ingredients decoratively on a tray and refrigerate until serving time.

Batter

1 egg
1 cup ice water

dash of baking soda
¾ cup flour

Beat egg and water together until light and airy. Add soda and flour and beat until mixed. Do not overbeat. Batter must be thin; if necessary add more ice water by the drop.

NOTE: Batter should be made no more than 10 minutes before using, and kept over ice.

Sauce

3 tablespoons dry sherry
2 tablespoons soy sauce
1 cup chicken broth

Heat sherry in a small pan. When steam rises remove pan from heat and ignite. When flame dies, add other ingredients; return to heat and quickly boil. Remove from heat. When cool, adjust seasonings.

To Assemble

Heat oil to 375 degrees F. Dip 1 piece at a time in batter. Fry about 6 pieces at a time, less if fry pan seems crowded. Fry about 1 minute until golden. Drain well. Dip fried food into sauce before eating.

TEPPAN YAKI
(Grilled Meat and Seafood)

Yield: 4 servings

1 pound beef steak	2 tablespoons soy sauce
1 clove garlic	8 large shrimp
1½ teaspoons sugar	10 to 12 fresh oysters
dash ground ginger	1 small eggplant

Thinly slice beef. Crush together garlic and sugar; add ginger and soy sauce. Use to marinate meat for about half an hour. Shell shrimp, wash well and remove black vein. Drain oysters well. Slice unpeeled eggplant into thin rounds. Lightly oil griddle; heat thoroughly. Cook eggplant, then add meat, shrimp and oysters. Cook until just done. Dip in sauce and serve with rice.

Sauce

¾ cup soy sauce	1½ tablespoons sugar
5 tablespoons dry sherry	dash ground ginger

Combine all ingredients. Stir to smooth.

The mud of the swampy morass that was early Chicago after prolonged rains made lasting impressions on visitors: "They (Chicagoans) were begat in mud, born in mud and bred in mud!"

SUKIYAKI
(Beef with Noodles)

Yield: 6 servings

3 ounces cellophane noodles
beef suet
10 green onions, cut in bite-size
  pieces
1 can bamboo shoots, drained and
  thinly sliced
1 pound mushrooms, cut in
  quarters
2 small onions, cut in quarters
½ pound fresh bean sprouts
1 Chinese cabbage
2 pounds beef steak, thinly sliced
soy sauce
sugar
sake
beef stock

Cook noodles in boiling water, according to package directions, for 10 minutes. Drain, cut into small pieces. Heat a heavy skillet; rub with beef suet. Add half of vegetables. Using high heat, cook until soft. Move to side of pan. Add half of the meat, in a single layer, cook 1 minute, turn and cook other side. Sprinkle with soy sauce, sugar and sake to taste. Add enough beef stock to moisten mixture. Add noodles and heat thoroughly. Serve over rice. Repeat cooking procedure with second half of meat and vegetables when ready for second servings.

Sushi are Japanese snacks or appetizers. Cooked rice is their basic ingredient. The rice is often mixed with sugar and vinegar and can be enclosed in seaweed and topped with cooked or raw fish. Other varieties are enclosed in bean curd or a thin omelet. Care is taken to make a tray of Sushi as attractive as possible by garnishing with greens, colorful raw vegetables, and other edibles.

CHAWAN MUSHI
(Seafood Egg Custard)

Yield: 4 servings

4 dried mushrooms
hot water
3 tablespoons soy sauce
1½ tablespoons sugar
4 small shrimp
4 fresh oysters

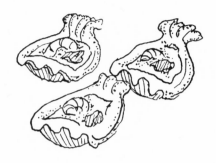

Custard

4 eggs
2 cups beef broth
1 teaspoon salt

1 tablespoon soy sauce
2 tablespoons dry sherry

Steep mushrooms in hot water to cover for half an hour. Preheat oven to 350 degrees F. Remove mushroom stems. Cook in 1 tablespoon soy sauce with sugar for 10 minutes. Shell, wash and devein shrimp. In each of four ramekins, place a mushroom, a shrimp and an oyster. Make custard by beating eggs and adding other custard ingredients. Fill ramekins with custard and place in a shallow baking pan. Add hot water to the pan to halfway up the sides of ramekins. Cover top of each ramekin with tightly fitting foil. Bake until set, about 20 to 30 minutes. Serve hot or cold.

KINOME YAKI
(Marinated Mackerel)

Yield: 4 servings

Marinade

¼ cup soy sauce
2 tablespoons dry sherry
2 tablespoons sake

1 teaspoon ground ginger
2 teaspoons sugar

Mix ingredients. Stir to blend.

2 fillets of mackerel, about 1 pound
each

Cut each fillet into four pieces. Place fish in a shallow dish and pour marinade over. Allow to sit for half an hour. Grill fish under broiler or in lightly oiled skillet for 5 to 8 minutes on each side, frequently brushing with marinade.

Garnish

2 green onions, finely chopped
1 cucumber, cut in sticks
2 tablespoons vinegar

2 tablespoons sugar
1 teaspoon soy sauce
dash of salt

Marinate vegetables in a blend of the vinegar, sugar, soy sauce and salt. Use to garnish fish.

For twenty-four years, the Japanese cultural festival, "Ginza Holiday," has graced Chicago's Old Town on the third weekend in August. The Buddhist temple is open for inspection and the indoor displays of flower arrangements, calligraphy, bonsai, sculpture and dolls are lovely. Outdoors, a large stage accommodates dance, drum, judo and kendo demonstrations. The food is the real attraction, however: chicken teriyaki and rice; sushi, a rice, seaweed, raw fish hors d'oeuvre; egg rolls, filled with Japanese vegetables; udon, cold noodles and onions in a soy-based sauce garnished with egg drops; and kintoki, sweet beans over shaved ice.

Outdoor merchants on Maxwell Street in the early 1900s

The Jews

In population figures, Jews are not listed as a separate group, because categories are determined by nationality and not by religion. However, it is believed that numbers of Jewish immigrants were included with the first surge of German immigration in the mid-nineteenth century. Evidence to support this is the fact that the first known Jewish congregation was initiated in 1847 over a store at Wells and Lake Streets. A temple was constructed in 1851 on Clark Street between Adams Street and Jackson Boulevard. Early records indicate that the little German-Jewish community lived on Lake Street.

By the beginning of the Civil War, many Jewish organizations and welfare societies had been started. A number of German-Jews fought as part of the German units from Chicago during the Civil War.

Although exact figures are not available, large numbers of Jews came to Chicago from the 1870s to 1900 to escape religious and political persecution with their Russian, Polish, Hungarian and German brothers. The Yiddish language was used to bridge the nationalistic gap stretching between them.

As the size of their population expanded, new congregations, schools and welfare institutions were established. New locations were sought out and one of Chicago's major hospitals, Michael Reese Hospital, was established on the south side.

The cultural and economic growth of the city gives testimony to the influence of the Jews who made Chicago their home. Countless and invaluable contributions have been made to theater, literature, business, industry and to the political development of Chicago.

Chicago Jewish food is basically a peasant cuisine. Although it retains the character of its religious origins, one finds strong German and Russian influences in some of the recipes, a comment on the origins of the Jewish community which census figures did not record.

Bride and groom under traditional Jewish bridal canopy

GEHAKTE LEBER
(Chopped Liver)

Yield: 10 to 12 servings

1½ pounds chicken livers
1 clove garlic, minced
2 tablespoons chicken fat

3 large onions, sliced
3 large, hard-boiled eggs
salt and pepper

Sauté livers and minced garlic in chicken fat. Drain livers on paper toweling. Sauté sliced onion in same fat, adding more if needed. Drain and pat with toweling. Put onions, liver and eggs through coarse blade of food chopper or chop in a processor. Mix with salt and pepper. Chopped liver should be the consistency of a semi-dry spread.

—Maxine Lichterman

CHALLAH
(Sabbath Bread)

Yield: 1 loaf

1 package dry yeast
1½ tablespoons sugar
1⅓ cups water, divided
6 cups flour

¾ teaspoon salt
2 eggs, beaten
1 tablespoon oil

Dissolve yeast and sugar in ½ cup of warm water. Sift 5 cups of flour and the salt into a large bowl. Make a well in the center of the flour and add the eggs, oil, yeast mixture and rest of the water; mix. Knead the dough on a floured board. Replace in bowl, brush with oil, cover and let rise until double, about 1 hour. Punch down and turn out onto a floured board. Divide dough into three parts and roll with hands into strands. Braid the dough. Place in a 9-by-5-by-2-inch buttered loaf pan, brush with oil, cover and let rise until doubled. Preheat oven to 375 degrees F. Bake for 55 minutes or until done.

—Ina Ostertag

HAHN ZUP
(Chicken Soup)

Yield: 8 servings

1 5-pound hen with feet, cut up
4 quarts water
2 stalks celery, diced
2 carrots, diced
2 onions, diced

1 clove garlic, mashed
2 tablespoons tomato puree
salt, to taste
white pepper
parsley or dill weed

Prepare the feet by scalding and skinning. Place them in water with cut-up chicken. Bring to a boil and skim carefully. Add diced celery, carrots, onions and mashed garlic clove. Simmer until chicken is cooked and vegetables are soft. Add tomato puree, pepper and salt and cook 10 minutes longer. Remove chicken and bone it. Strain the broth. Return chicken pieces to broth. Serve sprinkled with fresh parsley or dill weed.

REHTACH SALAT
(Radish Salad)

Yield: 4 to 6 servings

10 white radishes, grated
1 turnip, grated
10 black pitted olives, sliced
1 medium onion, chopped
3 tablespoons chicken fat
salt and pepper

Mix the radishes, turnip and olives. Sautè the onion in the fat until soft and pour over the radish mixture. Salt and pepper to taste.

SPARGEL MIT MANDLIN
(Asparagus with Almonds)

Yield: 6 servings

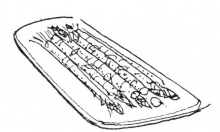

2 bunches asparagus, about 25
  stalks
6 ounces slivered almonds
½ cup clarified sweet butter
juice of one lemon
½ teaspoon crushed tarragon
1 tablespoon butter
salt and white pepper

Cook asparagus and arrange on serving platter. Sauté almonds in butter until golden; avoid over-browning. Add lemon juice, tarragon, salt and pepper. Swirl. Pour over asparagus.

LATKES
(Potato Pancakes)

Yield: 8 servings

8 medium potatoes
1 large onion
3 eggs
salt and pepper
¾ cup flour, approximate
4 tablespoons chicken fat or oil
sour cream

Peel and grate potato into cold water to prevent discoloring. Grate the onion. Drain potato; mix with onion, eggs, salt, pepper and enough flour to bind. Spoon mixture into pancake shapes in a skillet and fry in chicken fat, turning once. Serve with sour cream.

GEBACHTE FISCH IN MILCH
(Baked Fish in Heavy Cream)

Yield: 6 servings

6 haddock or cod fillets
1 large onion, chopped
1 tablespoon butter
1 cup heavy cream or sour cream

½ cup Swiss cheese, grated
1 tablespoon parsley
salt and pepper
white grapes

Preheat oven to 375 degrees F.

Place fillets in a buttered 12-by-7-by-2-inch baking dish. In saucepan, sauté onion in butter until transparent. Spoon onions over fish and dollop of cream over onion. Sprinkle lightly with cheese, chopped fresh parsley, salt and pepper. Bake for 15 minutes or until done. Serve with white grapes as garnish.

KREPLACH
(Meat-filled Dumplings)

Yield: 10 servings

2 cups sifted flour
¾ teaspoon salt

2 large eggs
1 tablespoon water as needed

Mix above ingredients, then knead until well blended, about 1 minute. Roll out thinly. Cut dough into 2-inch rounds. Fill each with meat mixture and fold over, pinching edges closed with a little water as needed.

Filling

1½ pounds cooked meat, ground
    (round or chuck)
1 egg, or enough to bind

2 large onions, chopped and
    sautéed
salt and pepper

Mix filling ingredients. Boil kreplach in salted water 12 minutes until they rise to the surface, stirring gently from the bottom occasionally to prevent sticking. Remove with slotted spoon.

Kreplach may be floated in chicken broth; or coated with a mixture of one egg, one teaspoon chicken fat and one teaspoon water, placed on a cookie sheet, well greased with chicken fat, and browned in the oven.

GESTUFTE KREUT
(Stuffed Cabbage)

Yield: 4 servings

1 head green cabbage
1 pound ground beef
½ cup minute rice, uncooked
salt, pepper, paprika
16 ounces tomato juice
4 tablespoons sugar
4 tablespoons vinegar

Remove 9 to 10 cabbage leaves and parboil. Drain. Mix beef, rice and seasonings. Slice rest of cabbage and layer on bottom of heavy pot. Take a tablespoon of meat mixture and fold cabbage leaf around it, securing with a toothpick. Place cabbage rolls in pot. Add tomato juice, sugar and vinegar. Cook over low heat for 45 minutes.

—Elaine Yapelli

LOKSHEN KUGEL
(Noodle Pudding)

Yield: 6 servings

8 ounces wide noodles
¼ pound (1 stick) butter, melted
1 teaspoon vanilla
8 ounces cream cheese
apples or apricots, fresh or canned
grated rind of ½ lemon

4 eggs
¾ cup sugar
1 pound cottage cheese
1 pound sour cream
graham cracker crumbs

Cook noodles in boiling, salted water, according to package directions, and drain. Preheat oven to 350 degrees F. Combine rest of ingredients, except graham cracker crumbs, in mixer and beat until pulverized. Butter shallow baking dish. Add noodles; cover with mixture. Top with graham cracker crumbs and dot with butter. Bake 1 hour.

NOTE: A variation is to add some chunky pieces of the fruit so that the mixture is not entirely smooth.

—Bess Desow

ASHKLIT
(Broiled Grapefruit)

Yield: 8 servings

4 grapefruit, halved
8 teaspoons butter
8 teaspoons honey
cinnamon
fresh mint leaves, chopped

Loosen the sections of the grapefruit. Place butter in the core of each and drizzle with honey. Sprinkle with cinnamon and place under broiler until bubbly and brown. Garnish with mint leaves.

PLETZLACH
(Apricot Almond Candy)

Yield: 15 to 20 pieces

1½ pounds dried apricots	3 tablespoons butter, divided
1½ pounds sugar	1 cup slivered almonds
1 teaspoon lemon juice	

Cover the apricots with water and soak overnight. Cook in 2 cups boiling water until soft. Drain, and puree in blender or food mill. Boil the sugar, puree and lemon juice to soft ball consistency. Beat in one tablespoon of butter. Pour onto a greased cookie sheet. Sauté the almonds in the rest of the butter, drain them on absorbent paper and spoon onto apricot mixture. Cool and cut into rectangles.

Purim is a holiday of great fun and rejoicing for children. Occuring early in the spring, it is a gala religious holiday in which presents are exchanged and symbolic foods are eaten. Playlets are given in the synagogues and Hamantaschen are eaten at home. The Hamantaschen are poppy seed pastries in the triangular shape of the wicked King Haman's hat. The children eat the pastry as a symbol of the downfall of Haman. Purim celebrates the end of bondage.

Birthplace of the atomic age

Boiled or fried meat-filled dough pockets are called by many names—*piroshki* in Russian, *fun goh* in Chinese, *ravioli* in Italian, *pierogi* in Polish, *kreplach* in Yiddish, *pastelitos* in Spanish, and are a staple Sunday meal throughout much of the city.

———————————

The first convention in Chicago, now famous for its conventions, was held in 1847. The purpose of the River and Harbor Convention, as it was called, was to persuade the Federal Administration to develop the harbors and waterways of the Northwest. In attendance at the convention was a newly elected congressman from Illinois, Abraham Lincoln.

The Lithuanians, Russians and Ukranians

Although each of these ethnic groups has intense feelings of individual nationalism, there are unmistakable ties which bind the Chicagoans who migrated from the three countries bordering Eastern Europe stretching from the Baltic to the Black Sea: culture, cuisine, and religion.

There were two Lithuanian families living in Chicago in the 1870s. Because of their inclusion with Russian population figures, it is not known how many Lithuanians were living in Chicago in the 1880s. It is known, however, that Lithuanians were living near places of employment at the stockyards and in South Chicago near the steel mills. By 1920, when the Lithuanian population numbered almost 1,900, churches had been built, small businesses were established, and the Lithuanian culture had begun to enrich the city which it adopted as its own.

By 1970, foreign-born and first generation Lithuanians in Chicago numbered more than 31,000. Although these Chicagoans have been absorbed into the ethnic mosaic, their individual nationalistic spirit is still evident in several Lithuanian journals which are circulated from Chicago, and in the Balzekas Museum of Lithuanian Culture which houses a library, archives and many art treasures echoing the cultural heritage.

Most of the early Russian immigrants to the city were Jewish. Like their German and Polish counterparts, they fled religious persecution in their native land during the latter part of the nineteenth century. They settled in the area centering around Madison and Halsted Streets and spoke the Yiddish dialect to communicate with other members of their Jewish synagogues.

The political upheavals in Russia in the early nineteenth century brought many White Russians to Chicago during the period extending from 1900 to 1920. Two settlements were established on the north side, one of them in the Wicker Park area. Shops and small businesses were established in both areas. St. George's and the Holy Trinity Russian Orthodox Church became the centers of worship. The latter is a beautiful church designed by Louis Sullivan. The Russian Easter celebration which is held in this church is attended by Russian and non-

Tower of Holy Trinity Russian Orthodox Church at 1121 N. Leavitt

Russian Chicagoans alike to participate in its moving yet colorful ceremony. By 1970, the Russian population of Chicago, including foreign-born and first generation Americans, numbered more than sixty-four thousand.

The Ukranians, too, were forced to leave their homeland in the early 1900s because of economic and political strife. In 1920, these Chicagoans numbered about 8,400 in the settlements which had been established on the near north and west sides. Like many of their neighbors, this group also clung to its nationalistic traditions, while making ethnic contributions to the city. Churches and schools formed a hub for activities, while service organizations and Ukranian language newspapers augmented nationalistic feelings. Although many of this ethnic group have spread throughout the city, the Ukranian National Museum, located in the center of the first settlement, draws these Chicagoans back to their beginnings with its fine display of Byzantine art, beautifully decorated Easter eggs, and other testaments to their culture.

The cuisines of these three countries share a lavish use of sour cream, whether it be as a garnish on soups, in meat dishes, or adorning the delicious pancakes fondly indulged in by all three nationalities. Cucumbers and sauerkraut are staples of many menus, and rich dark breads from whole grain flour form an essential part of this particular brand of ethnic cooking.

SABZI PIEZ
(Braised Carrots, and Onions)

Yield: 4 servings

6 scallions, sliced
¼ cup (½ stick) butter
2 tomatoes, chopped, seeded and
  peeled
½ teaspoon sugar
6 sliced carrots

½ teaspoon salt
good pinch of freshly ground
  pepper
¾ cup chicken stock
chopped tarragon
chopped scallion greens

In a saucepan, sauté the onions in butter until golden. Add tomatoes and sugar and cook until liquid is reduced. Add carrots, salt and pepper; stir in chicken stock. When mixture boils, cover and reduce heat and simmer for 12 minutes or until carrots are tender. Sprinkle with tarragon and scallion greens.

LASINECIAI
(Bacon Rolls)

Yield: 3 dozen

2 tablespoons sugar
¾ teaspoon salt
1 package dry yeast
½ cup lukewarm milk
3½ cups sifted flour
3 egg yolks
½ cup lukewarm cream

½ cup butter, softened
1½ pounds bacon, chopped finely
2 medium onions, minced
2 tablespoons butter
1 egg mixed with 1½ teaspoons
    water

Dissolve sugar, salt and yeast in milk. Place in unheated oven for about 10 minutes until bubbling and rising. Sift 3 cups of flour into bowl and make a well in center. Pour in yeast mixture, egg yolks, cream and softened butter. Make a stiff dough, adding more flour if necessary. Cover and place in unheated oven for 40 minutes until dough has doubled. Punch dough down, cover and let rise for another 40 minutes until dough has risen to double in size. Fry bacon and onions until onions are tender and bacon is crisp. Drain thoroughly, using paper towels to absorb any excess grease. Butter two flat pans or cookie sheets with the 2 tablespoons of butter. Separate dough into two equal portions. Roll each portion on lightly floured board until ⅛ inch thick. Cut rounds of dough with 3-inch cookie cutter. Place 1 teaspoon of bacon filling in the middle of each round, fold and seal edges over filling. Place rolls, sealed edges down, on buttered pan about 1 inch apart. Let rise until double in bulk in unheated oven for about 25 minutes. Preheat oven to 375 degrees F. Brush rolls with egg and water mixture and bake until golden for about 20 minutes.

—Aldona Remdzus Gallo

The Rookery built by Burnham and Root in the early 1880s is one of Chicago's most famous buildings. As legend has it, a temporary city hall stood on the site of the Rookery immediately after the Great Fire. This impromptu structure had a tower which became the home of droves of pigeons. The combination of the birds and unfair treatment at the hands of some city officials caused a complaining taxpayer to declare that "the place is little else than a rookery." Even the new structure could not shake the epithet.

AGURKAI SU RUKCSCIA GRIETNE
(Cucumber Salad)

Yield: 4 to 6 servings

3 cups sliced, peeled cucumbers
1 teaspoon vinegar
1½ tablespoons salt
3 hard-boiled eggs
½ teaspoon sugar
pinch of pepper
1 teaspoon mustard
½ cup sour cream
1½ teaspoons vinegar
1 teaspoon dill weed

Marinate cucumber in vinegar and salt in refrigerator overnight. Slice eggs in half and remove yolks. Slice whites into thin pieces and add to marinated cucumbers. Mash egg yolks with sugar, pepper and mustard. Blend in sour cream and vinegar; toss with cucumber and egg. Serve on crisp lettuce leaves and sprinkle with dill.

KUGELI
(Potato Casserole)

Yield: 8 to 10 servings

5 large white potatoes
½ pound bacon, diced
1 medium onion, diced

½ (5-ounce) can evaporated milk
3 eggs
salt and pepper

Preheat oven to 350 degrees F.

Grate potatoes. In a frying pan, brown bacon and onion. Pour over grated potatoes and mix. Mix in milk, eggs, and salt and pepper. Put in greased 2-quart pan, casserole or baking dish. Bake for 1 hour.

GRYBAI IR RŪKŚTI KOPŪSTAI
(Mushrooms and Sauerkraut)

Yield: 6 servings

10 dried mushrooms, sliced
1½ cups sour cream
2 pounds washed and drained
    sauerkraut
salt and pepper

Simmer mushrooms in ½ cup water until tender. Drain. Add sour cream to sauerkraut and simmer for 15 minutes. Add sliced mushrooms, salt, pepper and cook 10 minutes longer. Serve.

INDIEKA S VISHNIOVIM SOUSOM
(Turkey with Cherry Sauce)

Yield: 4 servings

1 turkey breast, roasted
1 .pound liver sausage or paté
4 tablespoons melted butter
1 pound cherries

2 tablespoons sugar
2 tablespoons water
½ teaspoon sweet basil
⅛ teaspoon cinnamon

Preheat oven to 350 degrees F.
Cut the turkey into four thick, even slices. Cover each slice with liver sausage and place in a casserole dish; do not overlap. Drizzle butter over each slice and heat in oven. Pit the cherries and place in stew pan with other ingredients. Simmer until cherries are pulpy; run through a food mill. Pour over turkey slices and return to oven for 7 minutes. Serve.

PIROSHKI
(Meat Pies in Butter Sauce)

Yield: 8 to 10 servings

4 eggs
2½ cups water
1 large mashed potato
3 cups flour
2 pounds ground round steak
½ pound ground kidney suet

1 slice bread, softened in milk and
  squeezed
½ cup water
salt, pepper thyme
1 large onion, chopped
¼ pound (1 stick) butter

Mix the eggs, water and potato. Add enough flour to make a smooth dough. Roll out and cut in 3-inch circles. Mix the beef, suet, bread, water, salt, pepper and thyme with hands until pasty but firm. Place 1 tablespoon of this mixture in center of each dough round, fold over and pinch together well. Place in 4 quarts boiling, salted water for 12 minutes until they swell and float. Remove with slotted spoon to platter. Sauté onions in the butter and pour over the piroshki.

—Connie O'Mara DeKoch

BITOCHKY SMETANA
(Veal and Potatoes in Sour Cream)

Yield: 12 balls

2 pounds veal, ground
4 large potatoes, boiled and
  mashed
2 medium onions, grated
salt and pepper

1 egg, beaten
4 tablespoons (½ stick) butter
1 tablespoon olive oil
1½ cups sour cream

Mix veal, potatoes, onions, salt, pepper and egg. Shape into balls and fry in butter and oil until browned. Add ½ the sour cream and simmer for 20 minutes. Add the rest of the sour cream and bring to a boil; serve immediately.

—William Ritis

KULEBIAKA
(Minced Salmon in Pastry)

Yield: 8 servings

4 cups sifted flour
¾ teaspoon salt
⅓ cup cold salad oil
1 cup hard butter, cut into small
    pieces
10 tablespoons cold water

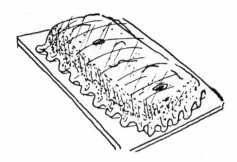

Mix all ingredients except water and beaten egg in large bowl. Using a pastry blender or fingers, work mixture quickly until coarse and granular. Add water slowly, mixing until a stiff paste is formed. (If dough does not blend together, 2 more tablespoons of cold water may be added to make proper consistency.) Divide dough evenly into two pieces. Sprinkle each piece with flour and wrap in foil or waxed paper. Chill until firm but not hard.

Minced Salmon Mixture

3½ quarts water
juice of 1 lemon
2 carrots, chopped
1 large stalk celery, chopped
3 medium onions, chopped
1 teaspoon freshly ground black
    pepper
3 teaspoons salt
1 cup dry vermouth or 1½ cups dry
    white wine
1 3-pound piece of uncooked
    salmon

5 medium onions, minced
¾ cup butter, divided
2 cups chopped fresh mushrooms
juice of 1 lemon
pinch of freshly ground black
    pepper
⅔ cup uncooked rice
1⅓ cups chicken broth
1 cup chopped hard-boiled egg
1 teaspoon dill weed

Place water in 6-quart saucepan. Add lemon juice, carrots, celery, chopped onion, pepper, salt and vermouth. When mixture comes to a boil, add salmon and simmer until salmon is firm to the touch (about 10 minutes). Remove the fish and remove skin and bones. Break into small pieces and set aside. Sauté all but 2 tablespoons of minced onions in ½ cup butter. Add mushrooms and cook until soft. Drain mixture and toss with lemon juice and pepper; set aside. Sauté remaining onions in ¼ cup butter in a 2-quart saucepan. When onions are soft, add rice and cook until rice is well blended with butter and onions, stirring constantly. Add broth and when mixture boils, cover and reduce heat. Simmer for about 10 to 12 minutes until all liquid is absorbed by rice. Combine salmon, mushroom and rice mixture. Add chopped egg and dill.

1 egg beaten with 1½ teaspoons water
2 tablespoons cognac

Roll one piece of dough on lightly floured surface into a rectangle about 7 inches wide and 15 inches long. Place on buttered flat pan. Roll other piece of dough into rectangle about 1½ inches wider and longer than first piece. Mound filling on first piece of pastry, leaving a 1½-inch space all around edge. Brush this edge with some of the egg and water mixture. Place second rectangle over first and seal edge. Puncture top dough with a ½-inch hole at either end. Pour a tablespoon of cognac into each hole. Refrigerate for at least 1 hour. Preheat oven to 400 degrees F. Brush remaining egg mixture over top dough and bake about 1 hour or until nicely golden. Serve with sour cream or lemon butter.

The Lake House, unusual as a brick structure in "the wooden city," was the first hotel in early Chicago to offer its guests such amenities as printed menus, napkins and toothpicks.

Lithuanian young people conduct a festival in early March. There are wood carvings, an art exhibit, and various types of handiwork on display. Lithuanian food is served to participants at the festivities.

VAISIU SAUSAINAI
(Date Cookies)

Yield: 8 to 10 pieces

1 cup flour
½ cup butter
¼ cup brown sugar
2 cups chopped dates

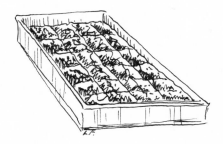

Preheat oven to 350 degrees F.

Mix flour, butter, and brown sugar together. Pat in 9-by-12-inch pan. Bake 10 minutes in oven; cool. Place dates in double boiler and add a little water (to form preserve consistency). Warm this mixture in top of double boiler. Spread over baked mixture.

1¼ cups brown sugar
2 beaten eggs
½ cup nuts

4 teaspoons flour
½ teaspoon baking powder

Mix ingredients together. Spread over date mixture. Bake 25 minutes at 350 degrees F. Cool cookies 10 minutes, then sprinkle with powdered sugar. Cut into squares.

Queen of the lakes

The Mexicans

In 1890, sixty-seven foreign-born Mexicans were living in the far southern reaches of Chicago near the steel mills. World War I brought many more Mexicans to Chicago in search of work in industry, construction and factories, to fill the jobs of Chicagoans who had left to serve in the military. By 1920, a new settlement had been initiated on the near south and west sides, and the total population of all Mexican-Chicagoans had reached 4,000.

Chicago's industrial expansion after the war brought more and more Spanish-speaking seekers of the American Dream. Between 1920 and 1923, the Mexican population had jumped from 4,000 to 20,000, making it the largest Spanish-speaking settlement in the United States, with the exception of the area of the Southwest which borders its homeland. Deeply religious in nature, the early members of this group had adopted churches and religious centers which had been vacated by earlier immigrant groups as ethnic locations shifted to other parts of the city. But, in 1923, the first Mexican church was established. Our Lady of Guadalupe in South Chicago, where the larger settlement was concentrated, boasted 8,000 parishioners when it was established in 1923. Organizations for mutual aid were established, and a seventy-five member *Banda Mexicana di Chicago* was formed.

Although the two original settlement areas still form the main neighborhoods for this group, reflections of Mexican culture can be seen throughout the city. Decorative murals reminiscent of Diego Rivera depict the cultural, religious and social aspirations of the Mexican-Chicagoan population. Colorfully decorated grocery stores and small cafes tempt the passerby. Several famous Mexican restaurants attest to Chicago's love affair with Mexican food, and the taco is rapidly joining the pizza as standard fare.

Mexican food is distinctive in its blend of ingredients and condiments. Food products which were indigenous to North and Central America have been subtly blended with Spanish and other European seasonings and ingredients, resulting in perhaps one of the most interesting of the Melting Pot cuisines.

Mural on Blue Island Avenue on the far south side

GUACAMOLE
(Avocado Salad)

Yield: 6 servings

4 large ripe avocados, skinned and
  pitted
2½ teaspoons chili powder
juice of 1 lime
juice of ½ lemon
1 garlic clove, minced
2 ripe tomatoes, chopped
1 stalk celery, chopped fine
1 onion, chopped
1½ teaspoons salt
¼ teaspoon pepper
¼ teaspoon coriander

Mash the avocado in a bowl and add chili powder. Blend in lime
and lemon juice. Beat the rest of the ingredients into avocado with
electric mixer. Consistency should be somewhat grainy. Chill before
serving.

MOLLETES DE CALABAZA
(Pumpkin Muffins)

Yield: 10 to 12 muffins

1 cup cream
1¼ cups canned pumpkin
1 egg
½ teaspoon cinnamon

½ teaspoon allspice
1 teaspoon salt
1¼ teaspoons baking powder
1¾ cups flour, sifted

Preheat oven to 425 degrees F.
Blend cream into pumpkin. Add egg, mixing thoroughly. Mix
spices, salt and baking powder with flour; gradually blend into
pumpkin mixture. Fill buttered muffin pans halfway with mixture.
Bake for 25 minutes.

TORTILLAS DE HARINA
(Flour Tortillas)

Yield: 6 servings

2 cups flour
1 teaspoon salt
3 tablespoons butter
1½ tablespoons lukewarm water

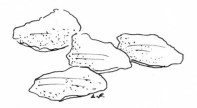

Sift together flour and salt. Cut in butter; add water and make a stiff dough. Turn out onto floured surface and knead dough for 2 minutes. Roll into balls about 2 inches in diameter. Pat each ball into a thin flat round, about 5 inches in diameter. Bake on lightly greased griddle, turning once. Drain on paper towels.

GARBANZOS
(Chick Peas)

Yield: 6 servings

1½ cups chick peas
1 teaspoon salt
¼ teaspoon coriander

2 tablespoons bacon fat
1 cup onions, chopped
⅔ cup red chili pulp

Put chick peas in saucepan with water to cover and let stand overnight. Place on heat and bring to a boil. Drain, recover with cold water. Add salt and coriander and cook vigorously over medium high heat for about 1 hour, stirring frequently. Sauté onions in bacon fat until transparent. Drain. Mash chick peas and add onions and chili pulp. Heat and serve.

SOPA DE LENTEJAS
(Lentil Soup)

Yield: 8 servings

1½ cups dry lentils
1 teaspoon salt
½ teaspoon pepper
⅔ cup tomato paste
½ cup crisp cooked bacon,
    crumbled
⅔ cup carrots, chopped
1 cup onions, chopped
1 dry bay leaf

Cover lentils with water and let stand for 6 hours. Drain. Put lentils in saucepan and add salt, pepper and cold water to barely cover. Add remaining ingredients. and cook gently over very low heat for about 1 hour and 15 minutes. Stir occasionally.

ESPARRAGOS CON HUEVOS Y POBLANOS
(Asparagus, Peppers and Eggs)

Yield: 8 servings

1 sweet green pepper, chopped
  fine
1 sweet red pepper, chopped fine
6 scallions, minced
1½ cloves garlic, mashed
5 tablespoons unsalted butter

salt
3 tablespoons vinegar
2½ pounds hot cooked asparagus,
  or about 48 spears
8 eggs, poached

Sauté peppers, scallions and garlic in butter until soft. Add salt and vinegar. Place cooked asparagus on platter with eggs. Stir sauce vigorously and pour over asparagus.

HUEVOS RANCHEROS
(Poached Eggs in Tomato Sauce)

Yield: 8 servings

2½ tablespoons cooking oil
2 cloves garlic, crushed
2 onions, minced
1½ cups green peppers, cut into
    thin 1-inch long strips
1 (6-ounce) can tomato sauce
1 (6-ounce) can tomatoes, drained
dash of hot sauce
1 teaspoon salt
good pinch of oregano
8 eggs
8 tortillas

Heat oil in large skillet. Sauté garlic, onions and peppers until soft but not browned. Add all other ingredients but eggs and tortillas. Cover skillet and let cook gently over low heat for about 25 minutes. Break eggs one by one into a saucer and slide carefully into hot mixture. Cover and simmer until eggs are poached, about 6 minutes. Serve each egg on a fried tortilla.

CHILE CON CARNE
(Meat with Chile)

Yield: 8 servings

2 onions, chopped
2 garlic cloves, crushed
1 cup green pepper, chopped
¼ cup olive oil
2 pounds ground beef
1½ pounds ground pork
1 (no. 2½) size can tomatoes

1½ tablespoons flour
1 teaspoon cumin powder
3½ tablespoons chili powder
1 tablespoon oregano
2 bay leaves
1½ cups pitted black olives, halved

In large skillet, brown onions, garlic and pepper in hot oil until tender. Add meat and brown thoroughly. Cover and let cook for about 10 minutes. Add tomatoes and mix together with meat. Blend in flour, add spices; cover and simmer for about 15 minutes. Add black olives and cover. Simmer for another 30 minutes.

PAELLA
(Chicken and Seafood with Rice)

Yield: 8 servings

1 4-pound frying chicken, cut into serving pieces
½ cup olive oil
3 onions, chopped
3 cloves garlic, crushed
2 cups uncooked rice
3 cups hot chicken broth, into which 1 teaspoon of chili powder is dissolved
½ cup white dry wine
½ teaspoon oregano
½ teaspoon saffron
1 teaspoon salt

½ teaspoon pepper
12 to 15 slices Chorizo sausage (hot Italian sausage may be substituted)
1 cup cooked ham, cut into bite-size pieces
½ cup cooked peas
3 (5-ounce) cans small clams, drained
1½ pounds cooked shrimp, peeled and deveined
½ cup pimiento strips

In a large heavy pot, brown chicken in hot oil. Add onions and garlic. Cook until vegetables are soft but not brown. Add rice, stirring so that all of the rice is coated with oil. Add 2 cups of the chicken broth and the wine. Stir to mix thoroughly. Cover and cook over low heat for about 20 minutes, until rice and chicken are tender. Mix oregano, saffron, salt and pepper with remaining cup of chicken broth and let stand while chicken and rice are cooking. Add sausage, ham, peas, clams, shrimp and 1 cup of chicken broth to chicken mixture. Cover and let simmer for 10 to 15 minutes more. Decorate with pimiento strips.

The Windy City

CHORIZOS
(Mexican Sausage)

Yield: 6 servings

1 generous teaspoon oregano
2 cloves garlic, mashed
1 tablespoon fresh paprika
¾ teaspoon cinnamon
½ teaspoon ground cloves
3 tablespoons chili powder

1½ teaspoons salt
½ teaspoon pepper
2½ tablespoons vinegar
1½ pounds pork, trimmed of
    excess fat and ground fine

Blend all ingredients into ground pork, mixing thoroughly. Cover and place in refrigerator for 3 hours. Remove from refrigerator and mix again. Shape into 2 long rolls, about 2 inches in diameter. Wrap in foil and keep refrigerated. The sausage may be sliced and fried without any cooking oil or butter. If properly refrigerated, it will keep for 2 weeks.

ANTE
(Cake Pudding)

Yield: 6 to 8 servings

1 pound cake, cut into cubes about
    2-by-2 inches
1½ cups brown sugar
3 cups warm water
4 egg yolks, beaten until lemony

3 tablespoons butter, softened
1 cup toasted almonds
¾ cup raisins
½ teaspoon allspice
½ teaspoon cinnamon

Arrange cake cubes in a low, flat glass dish. Dissolve brown sugar in water in saucepan; cook to syrup stage. Remove from heat and cool slightly. When mixture is lukewarm, beat in the eggs and butter. Pour over cake cubes. Top with almonds, raisins and spices. Cover and chill overnight. Serve with heavy cream.

The Middle Easterners

One of the most intriguing spectacles at the World Columbian Exposition held in Chicago in 1893 was the "Street of Cairo" exhibit. A number of merchants from the Arab countries which provided the exhibit did not return to their home lands, but decided to stay and settle in Chicago. Although exact numbers are not available, this small group represented the beginning of the Middle Eastern community in Chicago.

The reorganization of the Turkish Empire in the late nineteenth century had caused the displacement of many of its subjects. While many individuals remained in the Middle East, some began the migration to America and a few immigrants trickled into Chicago. Although many nationalities are included in this group, there is specific evidence that immigrants from Armenia, Syria and Lebanon began to settle in Chicago in the early 1900s.

World War I performed the *coup de grace* on the Turkish Empire, and soon immigrants from the affected nations began to come to America and to Chicago in larger and larger numbers. By 1920, the foreign-born and first generation population of Armenians numbered 1,028, that of the Lebanese numbered 200, and that of the Syrians numbered almost 500.

Many of these new Chicagoans opened food and grocery shops. Others dealt in fabrics and imported goods. Some with highly developed commercial skills moved into jobs with existing Chicago firms.

Chicagoans from Middle Eastern backgrounds represent a variety of religions, and many of them joined congregations of various denominations which were already established.

Although fiercely protective of their individual cultures, religions and political beliefs, there is a commonality among these nationalities demonstrated in their cuisines. Seasonings, methods of preparation and even the names of dishes constantly remind us of their intertwined origins. The food is delicious, with just enough of the exotic to make it a memorable eating experience.

Syrian mother and son

BATINJAN
(Eggplant Spread)

Yield: 4 to 6 servings

1 large eggplant
3 tablespoons butter
1 teaspoon sesame seeds

1 tablespoon lemon juice
1 clove garlic, mashed

Broil eggplant, remove skin. Mash eggplant. Add butter, sesame seeds, lemon juice and garlic. Mix well and spread flat on a plate. Serve cold as a vegetable or on flat Arabic bread.

JOBAN
(Cheese)

Yield: 8 6-inch cheese balls

2 gallons milk
4 junket tablets
salt

Heat milk to tepid. In a cup, melt the junket tablets in some of the warm milk; stir mixture into rest of warm milk. Let set for 20 minutes, stir again and let set for 15 additional minutes. Pour through a strainer. Shape the cheese left in the strainer into balls. Salt lightly.

TALAMEE
(Bread)

Yield: 6 loaves

1 cake yeast	½ cup sugar
3 cups warm water	½ teaspoon salt
2½ pounds flour	2½ tablespoons butter, melted

Dissolve yeast in ½ cup warm water. Place flour, sugar, salt and butter in a large mixing bowl. Add yeast and rest of water; knead until smooth. Set in warm place about 1½ hours until double. Cut into 6 sections and roll into balls. Cover and let rise 45 minutes. Flatten each ball to about ¼-inch thickness. Cover and let rise again for 40 minutes. Preheat oven to 450 degrees F. Oil a baking sheet and place dough on it. Bake until bottom of bread is light brown, then place under the broiler to brown top. It is best to bake only one loaf at a time.

SHOURABA IL KOOSA
(Squash Soup)

Yield: 6 servings

2 cups heavy cream	4 cups summer squash, cooked in water until slightly soft, then drained
2 cups milk	
3 tablespoons flour	
4 tablespoons (½ stick) unsalted butter	salt, pepper and dash of nutmeg

Pour the cream and milk into a large saucepan and stir. Dissolve the flour in a small amount of the milk and add to the saucepan. Bring to the simmer. Add butter, squash, salt, pepper and nutmeg. When slightly thickened, serve.

The oldest house still standing in Chicago, Clarke House, was built in 1836. It was moved from 45th and Wabash to its present location in the Prairie Avenue Historical Complex where it is being restored to its original glory.

SALATA IL SANE
(Tongue in Oil and Lemon)

Yield: 6 servings

1 beef tongue, cooked
2 small onions
2 lemons, juiced
salt and pepper

parsley flakes
1 clove garlic, crushed
5 tablespoons olive oil

Slice tongue into 1-inch cubes. Mix rest of ingredients in a blender for a few seconds. Place tongue in a bowl and pour the dressing over it. Chill 1 hour or more before serving.

SALATA KUTHRA
(Mixed Salad)

Yield: 4 servings

3 tomatoes
1 green pepper
1 avocado
5 scallions
1 cucumber
1½ tablespoons fresh mint, chopped

1 clove garlic
salt and pepper
4 tablespoons olive oil
2 lemons, juiced

Chop vegetables and mix in a bowl with mint. Put garlic clove in a press and squeeze juice over vegetables. Blend remaining ingredients and pour over vegetables. Toss and serve.

Traditional seasonings and methods blur as recipes are traded and handed around Chicago. For instance: cabbage leaves stuffed with meat and rice are *yubrak* to the Syrian, *holiskes* to the Jew, *golabki* to the Pole, *repollo relleno* to the Mexican, *gefullter kohl* to the Viennese, *verze ripiene* to the Italian, *golubtzi* to the Russian, *hvidkaal rouletter* to the Dane, *toltott kaposzta* to the Hungarian, and *mih shee mall poof* to the Persian.

KOOSA MISHEE
(Stuffed Summer Squash)

Yield: 8 servings

16 green or yellow squash

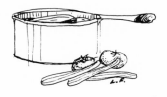

Remove insides of squash with a long vegetable corer.

Filling

1 cup rice (not instant)
1½ pounds boned leg of lamb, ground (use fat and lean, reserve bones)

4 tablespoons (½ stick) unsalted butter
salt, pepper and a dash of nutmeg

Combine ingredients and mix well. Stuff into squash, leaving about ½ inch of squash unstuffed so that rice may expand.

2½ cups tomato juice or tomato paste diluted with water

2 cloves garlic, chopped
salt and pepper

Place lamb bones on bottom of deep pot. Place stuffed squash cross-hatch on the bones. Cover with juice, add chopped garlic, salt and pepper. Bring to a boil and cook over medium heat 45 minutes to 1 hour until squash is tender and rice is cooked. To prevent squash from floating, place a plate over them as a weight.

—*Josephine Ghareeb*

SFEEHA
(Meat Pies)

Yield: 36 pies

½ cake yeast
1½ cups tepid water
¼ cup (½ stick) butter
¼ cup shortening, melted
1 teaspoon salt
1 pound flour

Dissolve yeast in water. Add butter, shortening and salt. Mix. Place flour in a bowl and make a well in center; add liquid ingredients and work together until elastic. Knead until smooth. Cover and let rise in a warm place until doubled, about 1 hour. Cut into 4-inch sections and let rise again. Flatten each piece by hand and fill with meat mixture as closed triangles or open-center crimped edged circles.

Meat Mixture

1 pound ground lamb
2 onions, grated
¼ cup freshly squeezed lemon juice

½ cup pine nuts, sautéed in butter
salt, pepper and allspice

Combine the ingredients in a large bowl.

According to which story you believe:

1. Chicago (Eschiagou) was named after the patch of skunk cabbage within which the city was founded;

2. Chicago (Che-ca-go) comes from an Indian word meaning great or wonderful;

3. Chicago (Chi-ca-gou) was named after an Indian chief whose tribe inhabited the area.

KIBBY
(Raw Lamb with Bulgar)

Yield: 6 to 8 servings

¾ cup cracked (bulgar) wheat
2 pounds lean ground lamb
2 large onions, chopped fine
salt, pepper, dash of allspice

½ cup pine nuts, sautéed
8 lemon wedges
8 scallions
½ cup (approximately) cold water

Wash wheat and drain of all moisture by squeezing it in a cloth towel. In a bowl, combine lamb, onions and spices. Add wheat. Knead until it reaches a smooth consistency, adding enough cold water to bind, if necessary. Form into a round cake and sprinkle with pine nuts. Serve with lemon wedges, melted butter and scallions.

LAHUM MISHWEE
(Skewered Lamb)

Yield: 6 servings

1 5-pound leg of lamb
3 large onions
1 quart yogurt

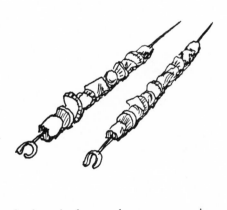

Cut lamb into 2-inch cubes and place in large glass or ceramic bowl. Cut onions into large pieces; place in bowl with lamb. Stir in yogurt until well mixed. Cover and let stand at room temperature for 4 hours or overnight in the refrigerator, stirring occasionally. Place lamb and onion pieces alternately on a skewer. Broil to desired doneness. Lamb is best medium rare.

INKHA MI BYTHOT
(Brains and Eggs)

Yield: 4 servings

1 lamb brain, about 1½ cups when prepared
butter
4 eggs, beaten

salt and pepper
dash of cumin powder
lemon or yogurt

Prepare brains by soaking in one quart of cold water for ½ hour; then remove membranes and boil for 15 minutes in acidulated, salted water. Cool in cold water. Drain, dry and separate into small pieces. Fry brains in butter until golden. Add eggs, salt and pepper. Let set on bottom, then scramble lightly. Turn out on dish, sprinkle with cumin and garnish with lemon wedges or dollops of yogurt.

—Yvonne Ghareeb

One of the highest holidays of the Eastern Orthodox Catholic Church is Easter. Traditional Easter eggs are symbolic of various aspects of the Passions of Christ. Red is His blood; blue is symbolic of the joy of Easter; yellow is the dawn of the Resurrection; purple is representative of the joy of the Resurrection. And the egg itself is a symbol of Christ. Eggs that have perfumes in their dyes (all taken from natural sources) signify the anointing of His body.

Edith Rockefeller McCormick, who once ruled Chicago society, required four men to serve at luncheons for two. Daily meals served in her mansion at 1000 Lake Shore Drive were accompanied by menus printed in French.

The Grecian Village festival is held in the late summer in Palos Hills at St. Constantine's Church. There is a raffle, and there are carnival rides and booths. An Agora is held inside the church (which sponsors the festival), where jewelry and Grecian artifacts are sold. A coffee house is connected to the Agora which serves cocktails, coffee and an assortment of the most exquisite Greek pastries: Baklava, Kourabiedes, Diples, and Melamaronaka. The other foods available at this festival are magnificently prepared. Spit-roasted lamb, shish-kebobs, gyros and lemon marinated chicken are served with a feta cheese Greek salad and rice.

Mexican Independence Day is celebrated in the middle of September. Two parades are held on the weekend with floats, bands playing Mexican music, horses decked out in fancy trappings and marchers in native costumes. A grand ball kicks off the celebration and it concludes with a ceremony at the band shell in Grant Park, with speakers, dancers, and singers. The celebration is robust, noisy and exhilarating to the participants—of which there are usually many thousands.

Feasting of the Killed Pig is a Slovenian event. It is held in mid-winter at St. Stephen's Church. The weather must be very cold so that the pigs may age a few days before participants gather to make sausages. After the pigs have been butchered and the sausage casings stuffed with the seasoned pork, a huge dinner is held. Slovenian dishes are served such as dumplings and kraut, delectable Slovenian desserts and the freshly made sausages.

The Poles

The social and political changes which developed in Europe in the mid-nineteenth century resulted in mass migrations to the United States. Many Poles, refusing to live under foreign domination, formed a large part of the ground swell of immigrants which reached Chicago during this time. Within the decade 1860 to 1870, the Polish community grew from 109 individuals to nearly 1,300.

The first Polish settlement grew and flourished at what is now the intersection of Milwaukee Avenue and Division Street on the north west side of the city. Like so many other nationalities which sought political, social and religious independence, one of the first endeavors of the little community was the establishment of its own church and school. The church, St. Stanislaus Kostka, was a small frame building thrusting an eighty-five-foot tower high above the low cottages and buildings surrounding it. For years this humble building, which amazingly escaped the Great Fire, remained a source of comfort and nationalistic pride to Polish-Chicagoans.

Early members of this community set up small businesses and factories which enhanced the growth of their adopted city. As their numbers grew, Polish settlements began to develop in other parts of the city, and new schools and churches were built. For the Poles, education and religion remained top priorities.

By 1900, there were about 60,000 Poles who were of foreign birth or first generation Americans. Nearly one hundred major businesses bore Polish names. One of Chicago's earliest institutions of higher learning, St. Stanislaus College, had been founded, and several national Polish journals had their headquarters in Chicago. Today, the Windy City has the largest Polish population of any city in the world, including those in Poland.

Polish food is as solid as the people who created it. Sausages, stuffed pierogi and fowl are mainstays of the menu, along with czarnina, one of the truly inspired soups of the world's cuisines.

Doorway to St. Stanislaus Kostka Church at 1351 W. Evergreen

BUCHTA
(Polish Braid)

Yield: 1 braid

1 package yeast, compressed or dry
⅓ cup warm water
⅓ cup butter, softened
2 tablespoons sugar
½ teaspoon salt
2 eggs, well beaten

1 teaspoon vanilla
2½ cups sifted all-purpose flour
water
1 tablespoon butter, melted
Confectioner's Icing

Filling

1 cup (5 ounces) poppy seeds
2 tablespoons sugar
1 tablespoon light cream

2 tablespoons corn syrup
2 vanilla wafers, crushed
1 tablespoon softened butter

Mix together all filling ingredients.

Dissolve yeast in warm water. Add 1/3 cup butter, sugar, salt, eggs and vanilla; mix well. Place ¼ cup flour on pastry cloth for kneading. Mix remaining flour into batter. Turn out dough on floured cloth; knead until smooth and elastic. Place in greased bowl and turn in bowl to lightly grease top. Cover; let rise until double in bulk, about 1½ hours. Turn out on floured cloth; roll into 20-by-12-inch rectangle. Cut dough crosswise in 3 equal parts. Spread each part with Filling, leaving ½-inch border on one wide side of each strip. Brush border with water. Roll each part from widest end to wet edge; pinch edges together. Braid the 3 rolls. Place in 9-by-5-by-3-inch oiled and floured loaf pan. Brush top with melted butter. Let rise until double in bulk, 40 minutes. Preheat oven to 350 degrees F. Bake for 60 minutes. Remove from pan to cool. When cool, brush top with **Thin Confectioner's Icing.**

Thin Confectioner's Icing

2 teaspoons butter, softened
1 cup confectioner's sugar, sifted

3 teaspoons boiling water
½ teaspoon vanilla

Add butter to sugar. Stir in water and vanilla; beat until smooth.

The city that works

CZARNINA
(Duck Blood Soup)

Yield: 8 to 10 servings

1 whole 3- to 3½-pound duck with
   giblets
1 package chicken bouillon
   (granular) or 1 package soup
   seasoning
1 large stalk celery, chopped
1 medium onion, chopped
1 carrot, chopped
1 sprig parsley, chopped
3 tablespoons salt
1 pound white raisins
1 pound prunes, pitted
1 cup flour
1½ cups duck blood
¼ cup vinegar
1 (5-ounce) can condensed milk
¾ cup milk

Wash duck thoroughly and dry. Place duck, giblets, bouillon, celery, onion, carrot and parsley in 10-quart soup pot. Cover with water and add salt. Bring to a boil and cook for about 1 hour and 15 minutes or until duck is tender. Remove from heat. Meanwhile, soften raisins and prunes by soaking separately in water to cover. When duck has cooled, remove from broth. Drain and reserve broth, discarding vegetables. Return broth to pot. Add prunes and raisins to broth. Cut up giblets and add. Beat flour, duck blood, vinegar, condensed milk and milk with electric beater until smooth. Slowly add mixture to broth, stirring constantly until thickened. Return to heat. Simmer very gently for about 20 minutes, stirring occasionally. Cool and taste for seasoning— more vinegar and salt may be needed. Serve with hot, buttered kluske noodles.

—Mary Louise Lantvit

The first theatrical performance in Chicago was held in the auditorium of the Sauganash Hotel in 1837. Master Joseph Jefferson recited "Lord Lovel and Lady Nancy" before his parents performed scenes. The "Jeff" award for theatrical excellence is named after them.

SURÓWKA Z JABTEK, MARCHWI I CHRZANU
(Carrot Apple Salad)

Yield: 4 to 6 servings

4 large carrots, grated
2 large apples, peeled, cored and grated
2 heaping tablespoons prepared horseradish, squeezed dry

pinch of sugar
½ cup sour cream

Combine all ingredients and chill.

BURAKI
(Sweet and Sour Beets)

Yield: 6 servings

6 beets
2 tablespoons flour
2 tablespoons butter
2 tablespoons sugar
2 tablespoons vinegar
1 cup cooking water from beets
salt and pepper
½ cup sour cream

Wash, trim and cook beets. Cool and drain them, reserving 1 cup liquid. Grate them coarsely. Make a roux of the flour and butter in a skillet over medium heat. Add the sugar, vinegar, beet water, salt and pepper, stirring until smooth. Add the beets and stir gently. When hot, fold in the sour cream. Serve.

SZPARAGI PO POLSKU
(Asparagus Polonaise)

Yield: 6 to 8 servings

3 pounds asparagus
5 tablespoons bread crumbs
4 tablespoons (½ stick) butter

salt and pepper
sugar, pinch

Wash asparagus and break off and discard tough part of stem. Lay asparagus out in a large skillet, cover with water and boil gently for 15 minutes until tender. Drain and place on serving platter. Brown the crumbs in butter with the salt, pepper and sugar. Spoon over the asparagus.

PALUSZKI
(Finger Dumplings)

Yield: 4 to 6 servings

2 cups leftover mashed potatoes,
  cold
5 tablespoons farina
½ cup milk
2 eggs

2½ cups flour, approximate
2 tablespoons melted butter
4 strips bacon, fried crisp and
  crumbled
¾ cup bread crumbs

Preheat oven to 400 degrees F.

Mix all ingredients except butter, bacon and bread crumbs, blending thoroughly. Roll into ropes on floured surface and cut into 2½-inch pieces. Cook in 3 to 4 quarts boiling, salted water until dumplings rise to the surface (about 10 minutes); remove with slotted spoon to buttered 2-quart casserole dish. Pour melted butter over them and top with crumbled bacon bits and bread crumbs. Place in hot oven for about 15 to 20 minutes or until bread crumbs are delicately brown.

PIEROGI
(Stuffed Dumplings)

Yield: 6 to 8 servings

1   3-ounce package cream cheese
2   cups flour
⅓   cup (⅔ stick) butter, melted
2   eggs
½   teaspoon salt
water as needed

Cut cheese into flour with pastry blender until the consistency of small crumbs. Add melted butter, eggs and salt. If mixture does not stick together, add water by teaspoons until a smooth ball can be formed. Rest dough and refrigerate for 3 to 4 hours. Roll out onto floured surface and cut into 2-inch squares. Fill with meat filling. Place water on all edges of dough and seal with fork. Cook in 4 quarts boiling salted water for 5 to 7 minutes.

Filling

1   large onion, chopped fine
2   tablespoons bacon grease
1   slice white bread, trimmed of
    crust

2   cups ground round or leftover
    meat
salt and pepper

Sauté the onion in the bacon grease until soft. Mix in the trimmed bread, which has been softened in ¼ cup water and squeezed. Swirl in the pan and then mix with the meat. Add salt and pepper to taste.

—Lorraine Dudek

The home of the skyscraper

BIGOS
(Hunter's Stew)

Yield: 8 servings

5 slices bacon, diced
1 cup chopped onions
½ pound fresh mushrooms, sliced
2 (no. 2½) cans sauerkraut, rinsed
  and drained
1 pound Polish sausage, cut
  diagonally into ½-inch slices
4 cups diced ham
1 medium apple, pared and diced
2 tablespoons brown sugar
4 tablespoons chopped parsley
3 beef bouillon cubes
½ cup hot water
1 cup red wine
¼ cup all-purpose flour
¼ cup cold water

Sauté bacon, onions and mushrooms in Dutch oven or large skillet until onions are transparent, about 5 minutes, stirring constantly. Add sauerkraut, sausage, ham, apple, brown sugar and parsley; mix well. Cover. Cook 10 minutes, stirring occasionally. Dissolve bouillon cubes in hot water and add, with wine, to meat mixture. Cover and simmer 1 hour. Make paste of flour and cold water. Stir into meat mixture. Cover. Simmer for 10 minutes. Serve.

GEZ Z KAPUSTA
(Goose with Red Cabbage)

Yield: 8 to 10 servings

1 8- to 10-pound goose
salt and pepper
1 garlic clove, crushed
1 large head red cabbage, finely
  grated
2 onions, chopped
1½ teaspoons caraway seeds
2 tablespoons goose drippings

½ cup water
5 slices bacon
2 tablespoons flour, generous
4½ tablespoons water
1 teaspoon vinegar
1 teaspoon sugar
½ cup dry red wine

Preheat oven to 350 degrees F.

Wash the goose, pat dry and rub it inside and out with salt, pepper and garlic. Place on a rack in roaster to cook, allowing 25 minutes per pound. Prick skin several times during roasting to let fat run out. Thirty minutes before goose is done, remove it from the oven and cut into serving size pieces. Keep warm. In a large saucepan, place the cabbage, onions, caraway seeds and goose drippings in ½ cup water and simmer for 10 minutes. Fry bacon until crisp, remove from pan and crumble over cabbage. Pour off half the bacon fat; add the flour to the rest and make a roux over medium heat. Add 4½ tablespoons water, the vinegar, sugar and wine; stir until thickened and add to the cabbage. Lay the goose pieces over it. Cover and simmer gently for 20 minutes, until goose is done. Serve.

SZTUKA MIESA ZAPIEKANA
(Beef in White Cheese)

Yield: 8 servings

3 pounds beef, roasted rare and sliced
4 tablespoons grated Provolone or Swiss cheese
2 cups **Béchamel Sauce** (recipe page 82), heated

3 tablespoons bread crumbs
3 tablespoons butter
parsley for garnish

Preheat oven to 400 degrees F.

Overlap the roast slices on a heat proof platter. Swirl the cheese into the hot bechamel and pour over beef. Sprinkle with bread crumbs and dot with butter. Place in oven for 20 minutes, until bubbly and browned. Garnish with parsley and serve.

In Chicago's early immigrant days housing was at a premium. It was not uncommon to have twelve people occupying three rooms and sleeping four to a bed.

CIASTO Z JABTKIEM
(Apple Walnut Cake)

Yield: 10 servings

½ pound (2 sticks) butter
2 cups sugar
4 eggs
2 cups twice-sifted flour
2½ teaspoons cinnamon
1½ teaspoons baking soda
4½ cups grated apples
1½ cups chopped walnuts
confectioner's sugar

Preheat oven to 350 degrees F.

Cream together the butter and sugar; thoroughly beat in the eggs. Add the dry ingredients and beat until smooth. Fold in the apples and walnuts. Pour into a buttered and floured tube or bundt pan and bake for 1¼ hours or until done. Remove from pan and sprinkle with confectioner's sugar.

—Louise Manke

The Chicago Polish community rejoices each year in the Polish-American Exhibit held at Navy Pier in September. The Exhibit lasts for three days and displays crafts, metalworks, paintings, and films of Polish-Americans. There are five restaurants which serve authentic Polish food with considerable atmosphere. A Polka stage and a disco stage provide entertainment for the participants, and strolling musicians keep the background alive with ethnic melodies.

The Puerto Ricans

Immigration patterns in Chicago during the twentieth century reflected a dwindling number of newcomers from Europe and an increase in immigration from other parts of the United States, Asia and Latin America.

Although this segment of Chicago's population does not spring from an immigrant group, its constituents being American citizens, the distinctive aspects of the cultural style of the Puerto Ricans have made a notable contribution to the ethnic patterns of Chicago.

Residents of this lovely island in the Caribbean, one of the Greater Antilles, began migrating to the United States as early as 1914, but it wasn't until inexpensive direct air flights between San Juan and Chicago were established in the mid-twentieth century that large numbers of Puerto Ricans began arriving in Chicago. In the aftermath of World War II, there were many jobs available in the Chicago area. The promise of employment and the bettering of their living conditions drew many of these new residents to the open arms of the city. By 1960, these Spanish-speaking citizens represented almost 32,400 of Chicago's population. Population shifts of early immigrant groups had left areas close to the center of the city open, and it was to these areas that the Puerto Ricans came. Many settled near established Mexican neighborhoods where the language barrier was not a problem. Others settled in various parts of the city where public and church organizations soon provided Spanish-speaking individuals to assist the newcomers in making an adjustment to a complex urban society.

By 1970, this newest group of Chicagoans made up almost 79,000 of the city's population, and settlements were concentrated in Uptown, Lakeview, the near west and the near south sides.

The cooking of Puerto Rico draws greatly on its Spanish influence; many of the dishes also reflect some of the exotic ingredients found in the West Indies. Chicago cooks are learning Caribbean culinary vocabulary in their attempts to duplicate some of the island's recipes.

Mural at 3300 W. North Avenue

TORTAS DE PLATANOS
(Banana Muffins)

Yield: 1 dozen muffins

¼ pound (1 stick) sweet butter
½ cup sugar
3 eggs, beaten
3 cups twice-sifted flour

3 teaspoons baking powder
1½ cups mashed bananas
⅓ cup milk, generous

Preheat oven to 350 degrees F.

Cream together butter and sugar; add the eggs. Sift the flour with the baking powder into the egg mixture. Add bananas and milk and combine by stirring. Do not beat. Fill buttered muffin tins ¾ full and bake for 20 minutes.

—*Martha Mack*

SURULLITOS
(Corn Bread with Cheese)

Yield: 20 servings

2 cups water
½ teaspoon salt
¼ teaspoon baking powder
1½ cups yellow corn meal
1 cup Edam cheese, grated
Achiote oil

Bring the water to a boil; add baking powder and dissolve. Add the salt and pour in the corn meal. Cook, stirring constantly until thick and smooth. Stir in the cheese and cool. Make into roll shapes about 4 inches long, and fry in the oil until golden brown. Drain on toweling.

PEPINOS EN SALSA DE NARANJA
(Cucumbers in Orange Sauce)

Yield: 6 to 8 servings

4 large cucumbers, sliced
2 tablespoons flour
6 tablespoons butter

1 cup orange juice
salt and pepper
mint leaves, crushed

Boil the cucumber slices in 1½ to 2 quarts water for 6 to 8 minutes. Drain. Make a white roux of the flour and butter. Add the orange juice and stir until thick; add salt and pepper. Place cucumber slices in serving bowl and pour the sauce over them. Sprinkle with mint leaves and serve.

NARANJAS RELLENAS DE CAMOTE
(Sweet Potato-Stuffed Oranges)

Yield: 6 servings

5 large sweet potatoes
6 large oranges
5 tablespoons cream
4 tablespoons (½ stick) sweet butter

2 tablespoons sugar
salt
4 tablespoons orange juice
1 orange rind, grated

Preheat oven to 350 degrees F.
Boil the potatoes in water to cover until tender, about 30 minutes. Cut the top off the oranges and scoop out flesh, being careful not to break skin. Peel the potatoes and mash with cream, butter, sugar, salt, orange juice and rind. When mixture is fluffy, stuff into oranges. Bake for 30 minutes. Serve.

—*M. Escorcia*

"One town that won't let you down"

CAMARONES GUISADOS
(Stewed Shrimp)

Yield: 6 servings

2 pounds shrimp
1 cup shrimp shell water
3 tablespoons salt pork, cubed
   small
1 tablespoon achiote oil
1 onion, chopped
1 clove garlic, mashed
1 green pepper, chopped and
   seeded
3 tablespoons ham, chopped
3 large tomatoes, peeled and
   chopped
1 pound potatoes, peeled and cubed
10 green olives, pitted and sliced
¼ teaspoon oregano
½ teaspoon sugar
salt and pepper
1 tablespoon lemon juice

1 tablespoon fresh sweet basil,
   chopped

Shell and devein the shrimp and set aside. Boil the shrimp shells in 2 cups water for 12 minutes. Strain. Reduce liquid to 1 cup. Fry the salt pork in the oil until brown and crisp. Add onion, garlic and green pepper and cook until onion and pepper are soft. Add the ham, tomatoes, potatoes, olives, oregano, sugar, salt and pepper and simmer, covered, for 15 to 18 minutes. Stir in the shrimp and cook until they are opaque. Swirl in the lemon juice. Place on a serving platter and garnish with fresh sweet basil.

—*Michael Escorcia*

Achíote (or annatto) oil is necessary for the flavor and color of some Puerto Rican food. It is made by melting one cup of lard in a skillet and cooking ½ cup annatto seeds in it for five minutes, or until they give up their color. After the seeds are discarded, the oil may then be stored in the refrigerator and used when needed. It will keep for several months.

OTRO MONDONGO
(Tripe Stew)

Yield: 6 to 8 servings

3 pounds tripe
1 orange, juiced
1 lemon, juiced
5 ounces salt pork, diced
1 teaspoon achiote oil
1 cup boiled ham, chopped
10 fresh sweet basil leaves
pinch of saffron

⅓ cup almonds, ground
1 tablespoon capers
20 pimiento-stuffed olives, cut in
    half
3 sweet potatoes, peeled and sliced
salt and pepper
3 green plantains

Place tripe and juices in a pan with enough water to cover and simmer until tender, about 2 hours, adding more water if needed. Drain, reserving the stock, and cut into pieces. Fry the salt pork in a skillet until browned. Add the tripe pieces and the achiote oil and sauté them. Remove from skillet and brown the ham in remaining fat. Return the tripe to the simmering pan; add the ham, basil, saffron, almonds, capers, olives, potatoes, salt, pepper and reserved stock. If there is not enough liquid to cover, add water. Cook until potatoes are done, about 45 minutes. In a separate pot, simmer the plantains in their skins in water to cover for 35 minutes. Peel and slice them and add to tripe mixture. Bring to the boil. Serve.

RES EN BROQUETA
(Skewered Beef)

Yield: 6 servings

Marinade

2 large onions, chopped
1 clove garlic, chopped
2 tablespoons butter
1 large mango, peeled, seeded and
    mashed

salt and pepper
3 tablespoons curry powder
4 tablespoons lemon juice
1 tablespoon brown sugar

Sauté the onions and garlic in the butter until soft. Add the other ingredients and pour into a bowl.

1½ pounds sirloin steak, cubed
3 ripe, firm bananas, cut in chunks
18 pineapple cubes

Marinate the meat overnight. Alternate the meat, pineapple, and banana on 6 skewers. Reserve the marinade. Broil. Heat the marinade and pour over the skewers which have been placed on a serving platter.

JAMON Y PLATANOS
(Ham and Bananas I)

Yield: 4 servings

4 large ham slices
⅓ cup shredded coconut
⅓ cup brown sugar
4 bananas, peeled and split

1 tablespoon lime juice
1 tablespoon orange juice
1 teaspoon cinnamon
4 tablespoons butter

Preheat oven to 350 degrees F.
Place ham slices in a baking dish; sprinkle with coconut and sugar. Lay banana halves on ham. Mix lime and orange juices and sprinkle over bananas. Shake on the cinnamon and dot with butter. Bake about 20 minutes.

JAMON Y PLATANOS
(Ham and Bananas II)

Yield: 6 servings

6 slices of baked ham
1 tablespoon Dijon-type mustard
6 bananas, peeled

Béchamel sauce (recipe page 82)
1 cup grated cheese

Preheat oven to 375 degrees F.

Paint the ham slices with the mustard and wrap one slice, mustard side in, around each banana. Place in a shallow baking pan and pour the béchamel, to which the cheese has been added, over bananas. Bake for 12 to 15 minutes until sauce is bubbly and golden.

PASTELITOS
(Little Meat Pies)

Yield: 24 servings

¾ pound ground pork
1 tablespoon butter
1 medium onion
2 small tomatoes, peeled and
    chopped
1 tablespoon chopped olives

1 tablespoon chopped raisins
1 clove garlic, mashed
2 tablespoons flour
salt and pepper
pastry for 9-inch pie
fat for frying

Brown the pork in the butter; drain off most of the fat. Add onion, tomatoes, olives, raisins and garlic and cook until onion is transparent. Sprinkle on flour, salt and pepper and stir until thickened. Cool. Cut 3-inch rounds from the pastry. Place 1½ tablespoons meat mixture on each. Fold over and pinch together, moistening the edge if necessary. Fry in 1 inch of fat. Drain and serve.

CERDO ASADO
(Pork Roast)

Yield: 6 to 8 servings

1 6-pound pork loin
3 garlic cloves, cut in slivers
2 tablespoons Achiote (Annato)
    Oil

2½ cups orange juice
2 tablespoons grated orange rind
salt and pepper
1 teaspoon oregano

Preheat the oven to 375 degrees F.

Make a pocket in the pork with a paring knife and insert the garlic slivers. Brown the pork in Achiote (Annato) Oil, then transfer to a roasting pan. In a saucepan, place the rest of the ingredients; bring to a boil and pour over the meat. Cook for 3 hours, basting meat several times.

ARROZ CON POLLO
(Chicken with Rice)

Yield: 6 to 8 servings

2 cups uncooked rice
½ cup achiote oil
2 frying chickens, cut up
⅓ cup lemon juice
salt and pepper
1 cup chopped onion
1 clove garlic, minced

2 cups tomatoes
2 large green peppers, cut in rings
1 bay leaf
1½ teaspoons chili powder
1½ teaspoons salt
2 cups chicken broth
25 pitted ripe olives

Brown rice in 2 tablespoons oil. Brush chicken with lemon juice and allow to stand ½ hour, then season with salt and pepper and brown in remaining oil. Transfer the less meaty chicken pieces to a large cooking pot with a cover to keep warm. Continue to cook meaty pieces separately. Add browned rice, vegetables, bay leaf, chili powder, salt and chicken stock. Cover and simmer gently for 40 minutes or until chicken is tender. Remove bay leaf and gently stir in drained pitted ripe olives and reserved chicken pieces.

—Dorothy Svoboda

When Her Royal Highness, the Infanta Eulalia of Spain, made her official visit to the World's Columbian Exposition in 1893, thirty thousand pansies were strewn for her path.

FLAN DE COCO
(Coconut Custard)

Yield: 6 to 8 servings

2 cups sugar, divided
6 large eggs, beaten
2 cups cream
1 cup coconut milk, canned
1 cup freshly grated coconut
½ teaspoon cinnamon

Preheat oven to 350 degrees F.

Place 1 cup sugar in saucepan and set over medium heat. Stir constantly until the sugar caramelizes. Warm a 2-quart souffle dish and pour the caramelized sugar into it. Turn the dish so that it is coated on the bottom and partially up the sides. Beat the eggs with the remaining sugar. Pour the cream and coconut milk into a saucepan and bring to the simmer. Gradually add the cream-milk mixture to the eggs, stirring constantly. Stir in the coconut and cinnamon and pour into the souffle dish. Place the dish in a pan of water and bake for 1 hour or until firm. Allow to cool thoroughly and unmold.

The Puerto Rican community celebrates San Juan Day in June each year with a parade. There are thousands of marchers and forty-eight floats. The sound of marimbas and steel drums crash through the Chicago air as the flower-bedecked floats and Latino motorcyclists precede a float representing a house made of real sugarcanes and candies. As the parade passes, chunks of the candy house are cut off with long machetes and flung to the massed parade watchers. A queen is chosen and then the revellers move to Humboldt Park where a mass is said. The festivities end with a dance.

The Scandinavians

The shores of the North Branch of the Chicago River near factories and mills provided the first home for the Scandinavian population. By 1860, they numbered about 1,300. Cultural life centered around the first Scandinavian church, which was located at Superior and Wells streets.

Although the Scandinavian group counted Finns, Danes and Icelanders in its numbers, it was the Swedes and the Norwegians who made up the bulk of this immigrant group from similar geographic and ethnic backgrounds. The latter two groups quickly took their places in the Chicago scene by adding their talents and cultures to the city's development. With their ability in construction work, they were readily pressed into service in the reconstruction of Chicago after the Great Fire. Gregarious by nature, the Swedes and Norwegians formed social clubs for both entertainment and charitable work. Many of these clubs exist today, their members the great-grandchildren of those early settlers. Swedish and Norwegian language newspapers were developed and gained national prominence in fearless support of justice and individual rights.

As the number of Scandinavian immigrants increased, settlements began to spring up in other parts of the city. These settlements reflected a concern for the welfare of the sick, the elderly and the orphaned. Two of Chicago's major hospitals grew out of this concern.

By 1870, foreign-born and first generation Scandinavians numbered 14,000. In 1900, Chicago was considered the second largest Scandinavian city in the world with 166,000 residents claiming ethnic origins from the North Atlantic. To this day, the Andersonville section of the city is one of the largest Scandinavian neighborhoods and is referred to with pride in its heritage and cultural traditions.

Scandinavian food is probably most famous for its uses of the gifts from the sea, but it drew from the available foodstuffs of the midwest in the development of delicious yet hearty meat and vegetable dishes. No Christmas is complete in Chicago without some of the cookies and breads which bear the unmistakable stamp of Scandinavian origin.

Swedish log cabin Museum in Andersonville at 5200 N. Clark

LIMPA
(Rye Bread)

Yield: 2 loaves

1 cup milk
1 package yeast, compressed or dry
1 tablespoon sugar
1¼ cups warm water
3 cups sifted all-purpose flour
¾ cup dark molasses

¾ teaspoon fennel seed
¾ teaspoon anise seed
⅓ cup butter
grated rind of 1 orange
4½ cups medium rye flour
1½ teaspoons salt

Scald milk; cool to lukewarm. In large bowl, dissolve yeast and sugar in ¼ cup warm water. Add milk and remaining warm water. Beat in all-purpose flour; cover. Let rise until double in bulk, 1 to 1½ hours. Mix molasses, fennel and anise seeds in saucepan. Bring to a boil; boil ½ minute. Strain, discarding seeds. Add butter and rind to molasses mixture; cool, then add to dough. Add 4 cups rye flour sifted with salt. Place remaining rye flour on pastry cloth for kneading. Turn out dough; knead until smooth and elastic. Place in greased bowl; lightly grease top. Cover; let rise until double, 2 hours. Shape into 2 round loaves. Place in 2 greased 9-inch pie pans. Cover; let rise until double in bulk, 60 minutes. Bake 40 to 45 minutes in preheated 350 degrees F. oven. Five minutes before bread is done, brush tops with warm water to glaze.

—William Johnson

ARTER MED FLASK
(Pea Soup with Salt Pork)

Yield: 8 servings

1 pound dried whole yellow peas
3 quarts water

1 pound salt pork, blanched
marjoram to taste

Wash peas; drain. Add water and soak overnight in large pot. Cover; simmer ½ hour. Add salt pork and marjoram, and simmer until tender, 1½ to 2 hours. Remove pork. Cut in slices and return to soup. Serve.

Many ethnic cooks make their own mayonnaise. Although seasonings vary and proportions of oil to vinegar may differ slightly, this is the basic recipe used.

MAYONNAISE

Yield: 1 cup

1 egg yolk
½ teaspoon salt
⅛ teaspoon pepper
⅛ teaspoon dry mustard

1 teaspoon lemon juice
¾ cup vegetable oil
1 tablespoon cream

Place yolk, salt, pepper, mustard and ½ tablespoon lemon juice in a bowl and blend carefully. Beat in the oil *very* slowly, ½ teaspoon at a time. When half the oil is in the egg mixture and it is thickening, the oil may be added more rapidly. Add ½ tablespoon lemon juice. When thick and fluffy, add cream.

PRESSGURKA
(Cucumbers in Sour Cream)

Yield: 8 servings

6 large cucumbers, thinly sliced
1 bunch fresh dill, chopped fine
1½ cups sour cream
salt and pepper
pinch of sugar

1 tablespoon tomato paste
½ teaspoon dried tarragon
2 tablespoons vinegar
4 tablespoons salad oil

Place cucumbers in bowl and sprinkle well with salt. Let stand 40 minutes and drain. Rinse. In a bowl, mix all other ingredients. Fold in cucumber slices. Chill.

BRUNA BONOR
(Sweet Brown Beans)

Yield: 6 servings

2 cups dried brown beans
4½ cups water
1 teaspoon salt
1 teaspoon lemon rind, grated

½ small onion, chopped
½ cup white vinegar
¾ cup corn syrup, dark
1½ tablespoons brown sugar

Soak the beans overnight in the water. Boil over medium heat for 1 hour, then add the rest of the ingredients and simmer for 1 more hour. Mixture should be thick and beans soft. If mixture is not thick enough, make a cornstarch paste and mix in. If too thick, add a little water.

FISKEBUDDING-HUMMERSAS
(Fish Pudding with Lobster Sauce)

Yield: 10 servings

3½ tablespoons fine dry bread
    crumbs
2 pounds haddock fillets
½ cup butter, softened
2½ cups light cream
½ cup sifted flour
4 eggs, separated
1 teaspoon salt
¼ teaspoon white pepper
2 teaspoons anchovy juice (drained
    from can)
Lobster Sauce
cooked seasoned peas
parsley

Preheat oven to 350 degrees F.
Generously butter 13-by-4¼-inch loaf pan; sprinkle with crumbs. Skin fish; chop fine. Beat in butter. In separate bowl, add cream gradually to flour; beat until smooth. Beat in egg yolks, salt and pepper. Beat slowly into fish. Add anchovy juice. Beat egg whites until soft peaks are formed; fold into fish. Carefully spoon into pan, filling to ½

inch from top. Cover with foil and set in pan of hot water. Bake 1 hour and 30 minutes. Turn out on serving platter. Spoon sauce over top. Garnish with peas and parsley.

Lobster Sauce

¼ cup (½ stick) butter
3 tablespoons flour
salt and pepper
2 cups milk

1 cup cooked cubed lobster
2 egg yolks
½ cup heavy cream

Melt butter; stir in flour, salt and pepper. Cook until bubbly. Add milk. Cook, stirring constantly, until thickened. Reduce heat; cook 10 minutes. Add lobster. Mix egg yolks and cream; add to sauce. Cook until thick, stirring constantly.

FRIKADELLER
(Meat Patties)

Yield: 6 to 8 servings

1 pound lean pork, ground
1 small onion, grated
1 egg
1 teaspoon grated lemon rind

1½ tablespoons flour
salt and pepper
½ cup carbonated water
4 tablespoons (½ stick) butter

Mix together the pork and onion. Knead until paste-like; add the egg, lemon rind, flour, salt and pepper; mix. Add the water and beat thoroughly until fluffy. Refrigerate for 1 hour. Shape into small oblongs and fry in butter until well done, about 3 minutes each side.

"That toddling town"

REVBENSSPJALL MED SVISKON
(Spareribs and Prunes)

Yield: 6 servings

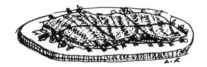

2½ cups pitted canned prunes,
    drained and mashed
4 apples, sliced thinly
salt and pepper
2 racks of spareribs (about 3½
    pounds)

Preheat oven to 375 degrees F.

Mix the prunes, apples, salt and pepper. Place one rack of ribs, curved side down, and cover with prune mixture. Place the other rack of ribs over the prune mixture, curved side up. Tie firmly together with twine. Place on rack in roasting pan and bake in oven for 1½ to 2 hours.

FRUGT SUPPE
(Swedish Fruit Soup)

Yield: 8 servings

½ pound prunes
¼ pound dried apricots
1 cup raisins
4 tablespoons tapioca
1 cup sugar

1 stick cinnamon
1 orange, sliced
1 lemon, sliced
3 apples, diced

In large saucepan, mix dried fruits, tapioca, sugar, cinnamon, orange and lemon. Cover with water, then add diced apples. Cook slowly 2 hours, until fruit is tender, or make in crockpot and let simmer 6 to 8 hours.

PLÄTTOR
(Swedish Pancakes)

Yield: 4 servings

2½ cups flour
¼ teaspoon salt
3 eggs
3¾ cups milk
3 tablespoons unsalted butter,
   melted
Lingonberry preserves

Sift together the dry ingredients. In separate bowl, beat the eggs until light. Add the flour to the eggs and beat to a smooth consistency. Beat in the milk and butter. Fry on hot griddle, turning once. Serve sprinkled with melted butter and powdered sugar and pass a boat of Lingonberry preserves.

JULA KUKA
(Christmas Cake)

Yield: 1 cake

1 cup sugar
1 cup butter
2 eggs
1 cup milk
3 cups flour

1 teaspoon baking powder
¼ teaspoon salt
¾ teaspoon cardamom
1 cup white raisins
½ teaspoon citron peel

Preheat oven to 350 degrees F.
Cream together sugar and butter. Add eggs and milk; beat. Sift flour, baking powder, salt and cardamom into creamed and beaten mixture; stir until well blended. Fold in raisins and citron. Bake in buttered tube or bundt pan 1 hour. Cool in pan ten minutes. Turn out onto a rack and decorate with powdered sugar.

MANDEL KAKOR
(Swedish Almond Cookies)

Yield: 4 to 5 dozen

¾ cup butter, softened
¾ cup sugar
1½ tablespoons flour
3 tablespoons heavy cream
1 cup ground almonds

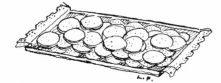

Preheat oven to 350 degrees F.

Place all ingredients in a bowl; blend together. When blended, drop by teaspoonful onto a cookie sheet which has been lined with foil. Leave space between mounds of dough for cookies to spread. Bake for 8 minutes. Remove from oven and let cool.

NUT KAKA
(Nut Cake)

Yield: 1 cake

2 cups sifted flour
2 eggs
1 teaspoon vanilla
2 cups sugar

2 teaspoons baking soda
¾ cup nuts
1 (20-ounce) can crushed pine-
    apple, juice and all

Preheat oven to 350 degrees F.

Mix together all ingredients, without beating. Pour into a 12-by-7-by-2-inch baking pan. Bake for 35 minutes.

Frosting

1 (8-ounce) package cream cheese   1¾ cups powdered sugar
¼ pound (1 stick) butter   1 teaspoon vanilla

Blend together until smooth and frost still-warm cake. Sprinkle with nuts. Serve from pan.

—Carol Ferguson

A major Swedish festival is held annually in Geneva at the end of June. Sidewalk sales attract the bargain searcher; quilt contests display the most elaborate of traditional quilting designs; and there are displays of scroll and floral designs on wood, and succulent sausages to tempt the visitors. Nordic dancers perform the folk dances to the delight of the onlookers.

In 1889, *The Chicago Morning News* commented on the gentlemen attending the trial of Mrs. Leslie Carter (actress), "Flashy young men known in common parlance as dudes."

Index

If you enjoyed *The Great Chicago Melting Pot Cookbook*, you will also enjoy other fine specialty cookbooks from Donning: *The Ham Book: A Comprehensive Guide to Ham Cookery* ($4.95 softcover) by Robert and Monette Harrell (the first cookbook of its kind exclusively on ham and its complementary dishes); *Savannah Sampler* ($5.95 softcover) by Margaret Wayt DeBolt (a classic on fine cooking in the Savannah area); *New Life Cookbook* ($6.95 spiral bound) by Marceline A. Newton (the only cookbook using the principles of the Edgar Cayce readings); and *The Heritage Cookbook*, ($4.95 softcover) edited by Marlin E. Foose (the ethnic cooking of sixteen nationalities in Tidewater Virginia). You can order directly from Donning (include 75 cents for postage and handling), or send for our catalog with wholesale and retail discounts.

Write to The Donning Company/Publishers
5041 Admiral Wright Road
Virginia Beach, Virginia 23462
804-499-0589.

WITHDRAWN